THE ENTREPRENEUR'S BOOK

ADRIAN FLEMING

The Entrepreneur's Book

Adrian Fleming
[publisher/imprint]

For information on reproduction please contact
Adrian Fleming
8 Charter Gate
Moulton Park
Northampton, NN3 6QF
United Kingdom

reproduction@theentrepreneursbook.com

First published 2014

ISBN: 978-0-9929185-0-7
(Printed)

ISBN: 978-0-9929185-1-4
(eBook)

*To my parents, David and Elizabeth,
my partner Alison, and Jimmy (our dog):
thank you for the years of support, and the
things you have taught me (yes, even Jimmy
has taught me things, as I will explain later).
Without you all, not only would I have been
unable to write this book, but also I would not
have had the personality, determination and
work ethic I make use of every single day
but I guess that's what makes me who
I am and that's why I do what I do.*

Notes To Readers

It is impossible to guarantee results, as Adrian Fleming is not working directly with you and cannot see, experience, react to, influence or advise on specific market, product or service factors that will have an impact on results.

This book and all associated materials are only provided on the clear understanding that Adrian Fleming and any other associated party is NOT providing legal, financial, accounting or professional services and advice. People reading and using the information in this book should consult the relevant professionals and service providers before applying what they learn from the book.

The book and associated materials are based on the experience of Adrian Fleming, and are intended to provide ideas, strategies, concepts, frameworks and examples that have been used, developed and learned over time. As such, these are intended to be beneficial to people who already are, or who are striving to become, an entrepreneur or successful business-owner; however, there can be no guarantee of success, and the information may not be suitable or applicable to everybody. The information in this book is not guaranteed or warranted to produce any specific results.

At no point is any warranty made in respect to the accuracy and completeness of details and information, even though all reasonable attempts have been made to verify the information provided, as things change over time. Adrian Fleming and all other parties associated with this book respect third party copyright at all times.

Adrian Fleming and all associated parties herewith disclaim any responsibility or liability for loss, risk or damage on a personal or business level as a direct or indirect result of any information in this book and associated material. The use of the information disclosed here is at the sole discretion of the reader/listener, who should, at all times, adhere to all applicable rules, regulations and laws applicable in the markets in which they operate.

Contents

Introduction

1. How do you know you are an entrepreneur? — 11

2. The four biggest things that cause entrepreneurs to fail — 21

3. The simple secret to a successful idea — 29

4. Taking an idea and turning it into a business — 39

5. How to make money – and how to lose money too — 47

6. The short cuts to success — 59

7. Learn to fail; do it often, and as quickly as possible — 65

8. Now is your time — 73

9. Communicating with your audience — 81

10. Don't let others get in your way — 91

11. What you must do next — 101

Introduction

Before we start on this journey together, I want you to know that this book is just the start of things, the beginning of your new lifestyle, and even though I'm not with you in person, I am here for you, and passionate about helping you achieve what you desire – so long as it's benefiting you and the people you sell to and work with too. You should always look to add value and help others first; trust me when I say that any other strategy for being an entrepreneur is not nearly as fulfilling, either personally or financially.

I also want to thank you for investing in this book. Even if you didn't buy it, you are investing your time, which is far more valuable. I want to make sure I give you as much value as I can in as short a time as possible, and also more than you expect – again, a key to success as an entrepreneur. So the first thing to do, which I know is a little strange, is to suggest that you go to the following website, where you can sign up for some free video training which, once you have gone through this book, will make things even easier to apply in your own situation. I'm not going to spoil the surprises yet, but as we go through this book together I will tell you what you will find on the website and how you can use it to your advantage, so head over to **www.theentrepreneursbook.com** and enter your details there, so I can help you get results faster and more predictably than I can just from the words in this book.

One thing I want to make quite clear at the outset is that I believe anybody can be an entrepreneur. Factors like money and education are not relevant – you will discover why later on. My journey started over 30 years ago; as I write this, I am 41 years old. Now I know you are wondering how my journey could have started at the tender age of 11, but it did, as I watched what was going on at home and got involved as much as I could. You see, I was fortunate enough to grow up in a household where my father David, was very much an entrepreneur. In fact his story, growing up in Glasgow at a time when things were hard, becoming a highly respected and incredibly successful businessman, due in no small part to his determination, work ethic, and the support of my mother Elizabeth, is far more amazing than mine. His and my mother's achievements, personality and support have, understandably, been a major influence in my life and have allowed me to do what I do, the way I do it.

I would also like to add that my parents' values, their upbringing, and also the way in which they have worked hard, and still do today (even though I wish they would take it easy – they've more than earned it) have all been a major factor in their continued success, making them who they are. Perhaps it's no surprise that others who grew up in the same part of Glasgow, at the same time, have also been successful; a well-known example of this is former Manchester United manager Sir Alex Ferguson, who has achieved more than virtually anybody else in his chosen field.

Simply put, success in any field, not just being an entrepreneur, is a skill that I believe anybody can learn and apply, and in this book that I have written for people who are or who want to be entrepreneurs, I want to help you discover what to do and not do, enabling you to get from where you are today to where you want to be, in the shortest time, with the least stress and at the lowest possible cost, both financially and personally. I want you to learn from my experiences, achievements, and more importantly, my mistakes, so that you don't have to make them.

When it comes to mistakes, trust me when I say I've made a few, which I will share with you along the way. However, something I have found is that it is possible to learn more from mistakes than you from success, and as such I encourage you not to be afraid of failure. Failure can actually be a good thing; the reality is that not everything you do will be successful, you will make mistakes and you will face stress and frustration, and these are the times when what you learn here in this book can really make a difference.

So my job now, is to help you identify opportunities and support you by giving you techniques, strategies and frameworks that enable you to capitalise on those opportunities and realise the benefits quickly, cost-effectively, and at as low a risk as possible; so let's get started.

CHAPTER 1

HOW DO YOU KNOW YOU ARE AN ENTREPRENEUR?

What I'm going to share with you is based not just on my own experience, but also on substantial research I have done. It concerns what I believe an entrepreneur is, and what it takes to successfully be that type of person. Being an entrepreneur is all in your personality: it's the way you live your life and approach not just business situations, but personal ones too.

My focus here is on how I can help you make more money, if that's what you want; but more than that, it's also about how to achieve greater results with the same or fewer resources, while at the same time being significantly happier with your lifestyle, as you stop trading time for money and start trading outcomes for income and the opportunity to make decisions on your own terms – in the end creating a win-win deal not just for you but for all involved in the process, including customers, suppliers and even friends and family too.

The systems I use and will share with you here work on both a personal and business level; for an entrepreneur the two are never that far apart. Most of the techniques I use don't require you to be an entrepreneur to benefit from them, but if you are, it will take your results to a whole different level, both personally and professionally.

What I'm about to share with you can be described as entrepreneurial training. No matter what others say, I believe anybody and everybody can be a successful entrepreneur if they want, and I will show you how and why.

Others may say that what I'm going to reveal is more about personal development; this is true to a certain extent, but I'm not going to suggest that you do anything other than what you are naturally capable of doing, because no matter who you are, where you live, what resources you have, your education or even your experiences, none of those things are anything other than historical details which have little or no impact on your future success; the reality is that there are people who started with very little who have achieved a great deal and those that were given every opportunity who wasted it.

What I do and will show you might also be described as marketing or trading; again these two elements have their place in being a successful entrepreneur, but they are not the only things you need to know.

I personally explain what I do and am about to share with you as helping you to develop as an entrepreneur; to me it's a "no brainer", because as far as I am concerned, having somebody else determine my income, my work hours, my lifestyle and what I do with my time is crazy and totally counter-intuitive; I'm guessing that you think that way too, which is why you are here and why I'm determined to do my best to help you on your entrepreneurial journey. I also expect that when as you see what's possible, and how simple it is, if you follow things step-by-step, it's what you will be doing without a second thought.

First of all, it's important that I explain my definition of an entrepreneur. It's not necessarily what a dictionary or even Wikipedia might say it is, but for me there is a guiding principle, and if you use it too, then there is no doubt you can achieve many if not all of your goals, and also perform personally, at the right level, day-in, day-out:

An entrepreneur is, to me, somebody who want's to "move the game on" – the "game" being any area that you are interested in. If you are not looking to invent, inspire and change expectations and possibilities, then you can still be a successful business-owner, but that's not the same thing as being an entrepreneur. You also don't need to be the founder of the next multi-billion-dollar business to be an entrepreneur. Money or indeed market domination are not necessary traits of being an entrepreneur; rather it's a behaviour, a set of beliefs, a type of personality.

People often ask if people are born entrepreneurs, as if being one is a natural ability, rather than something that can be learned. I say that there are three elements at play when you are an entrepreneur: a passion for something, the ability to identify an opportunity, and also the desire to take action. By embracing and refining those three simple elements, which can be learned by anybody, you will have a greater control over your own personal situation. Even if you already do some or all of those things naturally, they can always be improved upon.

Let me take you back to the time when somebody first asked you what you wanted to be. Perhaps it was a careers advisor at school, or a friend or family member. Well the answer that, as an entrepreneur, you should have given them was first of all to be happy, next, able to influence your own lifestyle, and third to be passionate about moving the game on. Conventionally, the name of the game is seen as the answer to the question; but that should never be the answer – just saying you want to be a doctor, an astronaut, or even famous, is not what you want to be as an entrepreneur; those are merely labels that people give to jobs, not a mindset and being an entrepreneur is a mindset.

Entrepreneurs like you and I aspire to being what I describe as "significant", inasmuch as we want to make a difference and to be seen by others as positively impacting something, or as I have called it, "moving the game on". I always see things from a different perspective to most others, and I want to help you do this too, because that is the foundation for entrepreneurship. More on that later.

I'm guessing you've already heard the phrase "The world doesn't revolve around you." Well let me just say that to me, this statement is wrong, and as an entrepreneur I encourage you to have the same view I do, which is that the world *does* revolve around you; it's the world that you see and engage with, and as such it has to revolve around you because the way you react, the messages you receive from it, the actions you take and the results that occur are all centred around you. You have the power and skills right now to make a difference to the world you live in and that's why everybody has a different range of opinions and belief systems. My version of the world will never be the same as your version, and that's why you and I have an opportunity, in fact many opportunities to, as I say, move the game on. Your world is what you are working with, not somebody else's.

Let me talk about this idea that entrepreneurship is a game, because I think that this idea is something you may benefit from, and games have certain factors that allow you to generate results that are predictable and replicable, a quality that is highly advantageous to somebody who's an entrepreneur.

I will explain what I see as the principles of a game, and if you imagine being maybe eight years old again, rather than whatever age you are now, it will help, because at the age of eight you probably acted differently than you do now, and a more mature version of this set of behaviours and natural actions and reactions will stand you in good stead as an entrepreneur. By the way, just to dispel a common misconception, age is not a barrier to being or starting on your journey as a successful entrepreneur, the story of Colonel Sanders of KFC fame testifies to this; he didn't start his world-famous "Kentucky Fried Chicken" franchise until he was over 60 years old.

First of all, games should be fun; if they're not, then as an eight-year-old you wouldn't play them. I strongly suggest that, even though you may never be able to have fun all day every day, nevertheless having fun and enjoying most of what you do is a good general rule to abide by.

My own version of the "having fun" rule is one that I follow as much and as often as I can, since it makes decision-making much faster and easier in all sorts of situations, so let me share it with you – and by the way, feel free to borrow it. My rule is that I will only do something for one of two reasons, or preferably both. First, I will do something if I want to do it, or second if somebody is paying me to do it, just like an eight year old. I prefer it when both these conditions are met. If you take nothing else from this book, then take this rule and apply it to what you do and I am sure it will change your life for ever.

Back to the games concept, if a game is not fun, then change the game you play, it really is that simple. The other thing to note is you don't need to play a game all the time, just when you want to. You can play more than one game over a given period of time; this way you can find out which one you like best and also which one you are best at. When it comes to being an entrepreneur, you don't have to give up everything, or focus on one thing only; try things out, see what you like and don't like, enjoy yourself. Here's a word of warning though; when you play, play one game at a time and give it a chance. To start with it's unlikely you will get the hang of something straight away, and secondly, just imagine trying to play football at the same time as chess – the likelihood of enjoying both games and getting the most out of each simultaneously is very low; and the same is true as an entrepreneur. Using this example in an entrepreneurial context, just think about the fact that you could decide not to give up your job working for somebody else, and use your evenings and weekends to try something new – this way you can see if you like it; but don't try to do something else whilst at you current job, because at best you will not perform adequately on either thing, and at worst you could get fired.

When it comes to games, you will have good days and bad days, and that's OK. Perfection is a good goal to have, but the reality is you can never achieve that each and every time you play. Your focus needs to be on minimising the impact of bad days and making the most of the good days; you can do this by working with a team of people (more on this later too), but your own performance is what you need to focus on, even if that's how you work with your team.

When it comes to individual performance, nothing beats knowing that you can always make improvements; you do this by learning from others, studying what works and what doesn't, using other people's expertise and experience as a way to greater results – and also by finding a coach or expert who inspires and gets the best out of you. In sport, a coach is not just expected, but is seen as critical to success. Entrepreneurship and business is no different, and those who embrace this tactic will get results faster and much more easily than those who think that the "school of hard knocks", "the university of life" or "trial and error" are the best and only ways to progress. The reality, as I have mentioned already, is that at some point you will make mistakes, and in the game you will lose at some point, but learning from this as well as learning from experts in your chosen area will help enormously.

There are two more game-related elements to consider. The first is fitness. Now in entrepreneurship, I'm not talking about the ability to run and jump, unless that's relevant to your chosen entrepreneurial game; no, I'm talking about mental ability, agility and capability, because being able to draw on these skills will get you through the good and bad times, and the greater your fitness level, the easier things will be.

And here's the last game metaphor, which by the way is potentially the most relevant and applicable: it's the fact that even though you must play by the rules, there's no reason why you can't work right up to them, maybe even change them if you like, so long as this is beneficial to you and all the other players. What I mean by this is if you can see a change that makes the game better, then make the change; this is the method by which you move the game on and gain a competitive advantage. Many experts and motivational speakers talk about modelling successful people, and while that's not a bad thing, I suggest that you see what other successful people do and then build on this with your own ideas – it's what I do, and what marks out an entrepreneur.

Don't be afraid of making changes, and by being confident as you make them, those changes will help you and those you serve too. The changes you make will actually be good for everybody involved, except maybe people who don't like change, but as we all know, those people are operating in an old-fashioned way that does not fit in to or add value to today's society, so don't let them hold you back.

Entrepreneurs are game-changers – not just players. If you are a player, then by my definition you are potentially a successful business-owner or highly valued employee, and that's OK; in fact for many people that's the right thing to be and there are things in this book that will help you to run a very successful and profitable business, but in my opinion your opportunities and results should not be limited by other people's rules and restrictions; that's why being an entrepreneur is far more exciting as well as rewarding.

Changing the game does not require a leap of faith or big changes; you just need to move the game on, even if only by a very small yet important amount. As we go deeper into this book, you will see why this matters and how you can exploit this on a local, national or even international basis, and why there's not a single market or niche you can't make money in as an entrepreneur.

Entrepreneurs come in all shapes and sizes, as do their results; just think about the founders of WhatsApp, who literally started with nothing but an idea yet in only five years, with a very small team of people, were billionaires. Equally inspirational and relevant, however, will be people local to you who have moved the game on; what they do may never be worth a billion dollars, but they wake up each morning with a real passion for what they do. So look for people with an entrepreneurial mindset, no matter what the business is valued at, because you may just find your next idea and game-changing plan from somewhere or somebody you least expected it to come from.

In the UK about 70% of all businesses are started from home not in an office. I'm sure in the United States and Australia the same is roughly true. The other thing, though, is that only about 20% of us are entrepreneurs, and that's OK, because this is why there's an opportunity for you. Also worth knowing is the fact that of those entrepreneurs, less than 20% make a success of it – and by success I'm not just talking financially here, but about the other important things, like lifestyle.

Many people start their own businesses to make more money and to have freedom, but most actually find they work more, have less freedom, more commitments and in many case less money than they had working for somebody else. It's an easy mistake to make, but also an easy one to avoid. If you want to be among the 4 to 5% of people that reap the benefits of being an entrepreneur – or better still, the 0.5% of people who *really* succeed, you need to have a strategy that incorporates a few basic things like innovation, a market understanding and also the ability to take action in the right way fast, that's what I'm here to give you. I want you to be in that 0.5%.

As this first chapter comes to a close, I have some questions that you can ask yourself, this way you can see if you qualify as an entrepreneur – and remember, it's OK if you're not, because many things in this book will help you even if you don't want to become one, but if you do have even the slightest thoughts of entrepreneurship, then this is the perfect way to harness those thoughts and make things happen.

I also want to make a promise to you. That promise is that I'm here to help you become the best and most successful entrepreneur possible, getting you the results you desire as quickly and efficiently as I can by sharing with you what I have learned and experienced. All I ask in return is that you use what I'm sharing to add value to others and that you use your talents in a positive way. What you are about to discover has taken me many years of hard work and thousands of pounds, maybe even millions, to formulate, and I would hate to see it used in a way that has a negative impact on your chosen market or on those around you.

Here are the questions, and just to be clear, you don't need to answer yes to all of them. In fact just one yes is more than enough at this stage.

> **Q.** *Do you recognise the need to do something, rather than do nothing, about your current situation?*

> **Q.** *Are you willing to take action and responsibility for your actions?*

Even winning the lottery requires you to take action, so thinking it will happen without action is naive at best.

Q. *Do you know or could you clearly define the quality of life you have now in terms of finances, personal fulfilment and a passion for what you do, and can you see that something better is a goal worth aiming for?*

Q. *Are you prepared, given the right tools and information, to look at where you are now and where you want to get to, and to segment that journey into smaller steps in order to provide yourself with an easily implemented plan?*

Q. *Are you prepared to accept that no plan should be fixed, and that along the way you will have to make changes in order to reach your goal?*

Q. *Do you have some level of fear or trepidation in making changes, while at the same time being open enough to appreciate that change is necessary and actually something that entrepreneurs, when they know why and how, can thrive on?*

Q. *Are you willing to not feel guilty for being successful?*

Believe it or not, this is a major reason why people don't achieve what they want or could, and is a limiting factor on their success both personally and financially.

Q. *Do you feel that in an area that you know or are interested in, you could add value to others and that, even if it required some external help, you could communicate that value to others?*

Q. *Would you be happy to deliver, or better still, over-deliver to your customers or audience?*

So now you know. An entrepreneur is somebody – no matter what their background, age, experience, goals, aspirations, financial situation, education, geographical location, dreams or even their chosen market – who "wants to move the game on".

All that's left to say now is…

…Let's play.

CHAPTER 2

THE FOUR BIGGEST THINGS THAT CAUSE ENTREPRENEURS TO FAIL

In this chapter I will only be giving you four things to take note of, but these things have taken me time to learn, and I will never stop improving the way in which I apply each of them to what I do. It's not that I didn't deep down know them, it's more that I wasn't able to simplify them and most importantly apply them well enough or instinctively enough to what I was doing day in, day out. However, once you know them, there should be nothing stopping you.

It's very rare to find an entrepreneur who hasn't had his or her fair share of failures. I know I have, and as we go through this book I will share with you what happened, why and what I have learned. My story is unique, but in principle it was the same for many a famous entrepreneur too, like Richard Branson with less-than-successful ventures like Virgin Cola, Virgin Clothes and certain other projects he has started. However, the key point, and the reason that so many venture capital investors like people who have failed and bounce back, is that they have learned from those setbacks, and the fact that it has not stopped them is actually an major strength.

Make no mistake: being an entrepreneur is about taking a risk. However, you can calculate the risk, which I will show you how to do. By calculating risk you can minimise it, but you can never eliminate risk altogether. Society changes, and risk is now present in situations where it was almost impossible to find only a few years ago – just think back to certain careers or public sector roles that once were described as 'jobs for life'; things have changed and you and I have no control over them, so being able to determine your own destiny is no bad thing, you do this by being an entrepreneur.

The other side of the coin is that with risk comes reward. Now you have the opportunity to be passionate about something, and with the help of this book you may benefit from what I have done and learned along the way. In fact in writing this book I wanted to create what I would have liked to have been given when I started out, rather than having to find things out for myself the hard way.

Too many entrepreneurs apply what they think is logic, but is actually better described as "throwing mud at the wall to see what sticks", as a technique to find out what works and what doesn't. I know I used to use this technique, but it's very wasteful, stressful, hard work, expensive and not very systematic. Systems, formulas and frameworks are the key to your continued success.

It's not uncommon to see once-successful people "fall from grace", and I feel that is often as a result of not having the right systems in place.

Personally, I have worked across business-to-business and business-to-consumer marketing, advertising and PR projects for over 20 years, in areas as diverse as toys to construction, industrial adhesives to fashion and for companies that have ranged from small start-up entrepreneurial dot.com businesses looking to raise funds for an idea, through to global and Fortune 500 organisations.

I'm a serial entrepreneur at heart who lives in the UK but has also lived in the United States. I've always been dynamic and ready to have a go at almost anything, and like many people I have learned from and look up to, was influenced in the early 1990s by Tony Robbins. I remember at the age of just 20, when I lived on my own in the States, watching his infomercials, buying the audio cassettes (yes, this was how they were supplied – CDs were around but not so common), and listening to them on the way to and from work.

I also remember walking across burning hot coals at one of Tony Robbins' "Unleash The Power Within" seminars in Massachusetts at the age of 20 or 21 at the end of the first evening. Tony's seminar started on the Friday afternoon, and being from the UK I found the style of the event quite alien – we Brits are much quieter and more reserved (but as they say, "It's the quite ones you have to watch out for"). "Unleash The Power Within" events were much smaller than they are today; you even had your picture taken as you walked across the hot coals. I still have that picture, and when the evening was over I remember chatting to Tony as we walked back to the hotel. That seminar definitely had a profound impact on me, so much so that a few years ago I repeated the experience at a massive event with thousands of people at the Excel centre in London with my partner Alison. She also has great and positive memories of the event, and those have helped her, as she too is an entrepreneur, specialising in fashion, so appreciates what you can achieve if you put your mind to it. I share this story with you because I want you to realise that, even though I highly recommend attending "Unleash The Power Within" if you get a chance, you don't need to walk across hot coals as Alison and I, and countless others have done, but you do need to push yourself to do things that you may feel are outside of your comfort zone from time to time, because that's when remarkable things occur.

I have worked and continue to work across the world on projects and opportunities, and in my experience it's having the right system and framework that delivers results each and every time, not the subject, market, country or even the product or service. I have all sorts of entrepreneurial interests, from my core expertise of cross-media marketing, to having owned and published magazines; I now make a very nice income from this. I have commercial and residential property interests, I have developed the strategy behind technology platforms, mobile apps and software, and have brought them to market; I help design and produce physical products, which are made in places as far away as China, and I have even built a TV and entertainment model that I will talk about later on in this book that has yet to be delivered but, long story short, I managed to get to the point where a letter of intent was signed for an initial investment of over $10 million.

Over the years I have invested in not just my own ideas and projects, but those of others , so I know what the risks and rewards are like on a very personal level for other people. It's not just about risking money, however; even though there have been companies I have worked with, and invested in too, that haven't made it, I have learnt more from those than when things work out. One thing I can say however, is that when things start to "go wrong", I have been able to identify them in advance, and when I am not in control of the business, just an investor or advisor, I have been able to "come out", in almost every instance, with a profit or at the very least breaking even financially, even when very shortly afterwards the business has closed. Real entrepreneurship and investment, at least from my point of view, is nothing like TV shows such as "Dragon's Den" here in the UK, or "Shark Tank" in the United States, suggest; such shows are just promotional vehicles for the products, services, presenters and investors, and this could be useful, but what I'm going to share and what you need, are actionable strategies.

I continue to work with successful, highly profitable and established businesses and the entrepreneurial elements and challenges may be slightly different but the solutions are almost always the same, so once you know them it's far more straightforward. I'm not going to say easy, because being an entrepreneur is never easy.

I'm regularly asked by others to offer my advice or opinions and to get involved in helping develop ideas into businesses. The types of business and people I have helped range from individuals with a passion and no money, to companies with multi-million pound venture capital funding, and one thing I am certain of is that success has little, if anything, to do with the initial financing; in fact sometimes having easy access to money can be a danger.

Entrepreneurial ideas and businesses seem to come my way on a regular basis; I guess that's because I have built up a reputation with those that know me, as somebody who can make things happen, who knows his subjects and will also work diligently. Very recently I was asked to meet with three people, one who I knew and two who I did not, to see if I would work with them to help take a very clever and patented piece of technology to market; all three people involved have an impressive track record in business and are really nice people , but this leads me in to the first thing that can cause entrepreneurs to fail, and that's not knowing when to say no.

As an entrepreneur, I suffer from the fact that I am constantly coming up with ideas, even in subject areas I know little about, in fact I love looking at a market, product or service and applying my skills to look for opportunities that exist; if there was only one thing I could do all day, that would be it. Some people say, I'm a "business magpie", because I'm attracted to "shiny objects". (If you don't have magpies where you live, they are black and white birds that are thought to be not just the smartest birds, but among the most intelligent of all animals; however, they are easily distracted by shiny new things, which they like to collect.) It's all too easy as an entrepreneur to have this problem. In a business context, this doesn't mean liking actually shiny objects, although anybody that knows me will tell you that I have a passion for nice cars and watches too, but I use this as a metaphor for opportunities. Because as an entrepreneur you are able to see opportunities when others don't, and are naturally dynamic, it's hard to not act on them; but just as with the game analogy earlier, you need to play one game at a time if you want the results, so you have to focus on one opportunity at a time.

The second thing that causes entrepreneurs to fail is that they fail to innovate. In markets today you must constantly innovate if you want to have a sustainable and successful business. Product life cycles are very, very short; in fact in many cases now you have less than six months to capitalise on an innovation, because of the speed and ease with which products can be superseded. Although lack of innovation is a major cause of failure, don't worry; I'm going to show you exactly how you can continue to innovate in your chosen area, and also how to differentiate yourself from the competition.

The third major cause of failure is a lack of effective marketing. The reality is that success is not just about having the best product or service, or the lowest cost or lowest selling price. Success or failure depends on how well you define your target market and then strategically educate the market on how you can provide what's wanted. Most importantly, over and above the initial marketing and education, because you want a long-term and profitable business that allows you to be an entrepreneur, you must provide what customers need – not just what they want – even if they don't know what they need to start with. This way they will actually get the results they want, and then become supporters and fans of your work.

Last but not least, the fourth major cause of failure is perfectionism, and this is often the hardest one to overcome. As an entrepreneur, you will want to do the very best you can in everything you do; however, you have to get products and services launched, and waiting until you have something that you feel is 100% right before you do this will only result in one thing, not launching. I have seen this problem occur to products and services that I have created, and I have watched people I advise make this mistake too. In my opinion, if you have a product or service that you are more than 65% happy with and is fit for purpose, it's time to get selling, because this will help you in two ways: first of all, it gives you clarity on whether the market actually wants the product or service (and, by the way, if you need to make small changes, you can do so at this stage much more easily than later). Secondly, starting to sell sooner rather than later also generates revenue, and there is no better way to stay motivated than knowing the thing you are passionate about is accepted and being bought by others.

There are some people who even suggest (and this is no bad thing, even if it's not something I do personally) planning out your idea, putting together a sales presentation and starting selling before you actually have anything like a deliverable product or service. If that's not your style, then you can go one stage further and use samples to sell from, but never, ever feel you have to have a perfect or even any more than 80% correct product or service to make a success of what you are doing. Going to market faster gives you the ability to make more money too over time, through one of the other potential failure points, innovation. I will explain all about this in a few chapters' time.

Just to recap, potential failure reason number one is not focusing on one opportunity at a time. The second cause of failure is not continually innovating. The third point of failure is not making sure your marketing is effective, and the fourth reason people fail is that they prefer to delay starting to sell until they have created the perfect product or service.

Just knowing, at this early stage, that having one, two or three of these elements right, without the other or others in place will lead to reduced results, or worse still failure, gives you a competitive advantage. You needn't worry about them for now, as these elements are things that I will return to and deal with in detail, as we progress together.

CHAPTER 3
THE SIMPLE SECRET TO A SUCCESSFUL IDEA

No matter what anybody tells you, you don't need permission to be or become an entrepreneur. If being an entrepreneur is something of interest to you, then all you need to do is come up with a few ideas to start with, but the question that always seems to come up and that I'm asked is: "What should I do?" Now there is no way I can say from this book exactly what you should do, even if we were sat together it wouldn't be a simple question to answer, but I'm going to do my best to make it as easy and clear as I can for you.

The easiest way to be successful as an entrepreneur is to solve a problem for somebody; the bigger the problem, socially, financially or both, the bigger your window for success, it's as simple as that, because by finding a solution you are moving the game on.

All too often, people seem to want to convert their hobby into a business. This is a great concept, but it's not always realistic or the right thing to do, unless of course you can move the game on in that area. But before we go into too much detail, let's look at the logic and planning that go into coming up with a successful idea, and also some of the misconceptions and problems that others think exist, but in reality don't, or at least don't have to.

Remember earlier on I talked about the fact that being an entrepreneur is a mindset and a personality, so one of the best things you can do right now is dispel what are termed, "limiting beliefs", because as you appreciate, if you fail to take action and move from where you are now to where you want to get to, nothing changes, so let me first go through some of the common misconceptions and limiting beliefs. That way, we can sort things out right now.

People think you should work hard now to get rewards later – WRONG.

There is no reason at all why you can't get the rewards now, or at the very least quickly, and there are no guarantees that working hard now will allow you to take it easy and have fun later anyway, for all sorts of reasons outside of your control, so make the decision to do something now. Being an entrepreneur, of course you should work hard, but get the rewards from your work now as well as later. A word of warning though, or should I say common sense: you have to look for the rewards in areas other than just monetary income at the outset, because that's not where your rewards will come from initially. As I will explain later, you will not make a fortune, or at least you are highly unlikely to make a fortune to start with, but this, if you have the right mindset, will not be a problem.

Following on from the first misconception, it's said that work is not something you enjoy – WRONG.

If you are not enjoying what you do, and I know that many people don't have this in their lives, then make changes now. I am not for one minute going to suggest that you have to enjoy working every hour of every day, but later on I will share some ideas on how to do more of this and less of the things you don't like doing. My advice is that the day you wake up and don't feel at all enthusiastic about work, or you do the bare minimum to get through what's required of you, is the day you need to question what you are doing and, I would suggest, make changes.

Next comes the idea that it's safer to work for somebody else – WRONG.

I talked about this earlier and you will see later on why. As time passes, the risks facing employees increase because of technology and market conditions, so don't let somebody else define your employment status – or your income either, for that matter.

Here comes another big roadblock to people acting on their entrepreneurial instincts, and that's the belief that you need certain qualifications or expertise – REALLY WRONG.

This belief is an out-of-date concept that others would like you to believe, because it suits them. Qualifications and expertise are NOT prerequisites for success, for example I personally know more multimillionaires without a university degree than with one. I am not saying education isn't important – I was very fortunate to have had an exceptionally good education, but my entrepreneurial spirit and ideas didn't come from a classroom or lecture theatre, and my skills were learned and practised outside of that environment too; that's why I know you can do it, and in Chapter 6 I will share with you more on this.

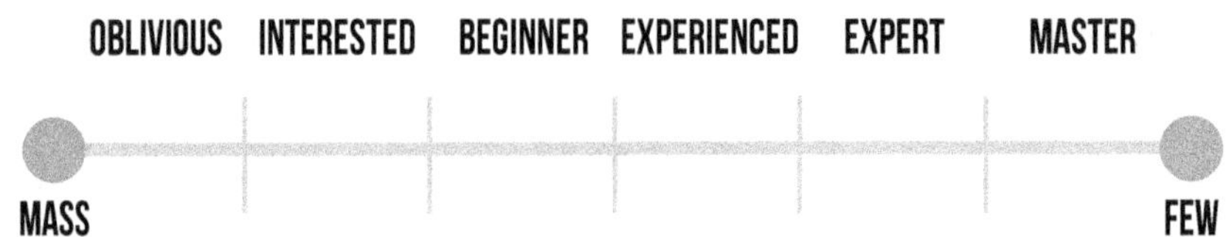

This simple diagram could be one of the most important parts of this book if you are concerned about your education or expertise preventing you from being an entrepreneur.

The fact of the matter is you only need to be one or more stages on from the market and the people you are serving in order to be successful. If you are providing a service to people who are beginners, then so long as you are experienced, you will be able to add value to those beginners, and the great thing is that over time, you can move along what I call the ability line, keeping ahead of your customers so you can continue to provide value to them as they progress. This is a very clever and profitable tactic.

The same rules apply if you want to be of value to an expert; in that case you have to be a master, and because as ability increases, the number of people able to serve that community falls, you can charge more for what you provide too, if you desire. If you want a simple example of this framework in action, think about what happens if, for example, you were learning a martial art. I know when I first learned martial arts I was taught by and learned from experienced people, rather than experts, but as I progressed, gaining new skills, confidence and colours of belt to signify my ability, I needed more skilled instruction, and this came from experts and masters.

Because I know the strategy is an essential one to understand, and I want to do all I can to help you, I have created a training video for you in the online area you can access at **www.theentrepreneursbook.com**. I highly recommend that once you have finished reading this chapter, you go and watch the video, as it is the best way for me to explain the simple but powerful concept and it will enable you to develop your ideas and skills to provide an ongoing profit stream, not just a one-off sale.

Next in the list of misconceptions comes the feeling that you need money, or need to raise money, to be an entrepreneur – WRONG.

Just yesterday I was shown statistics from here in the UK that were gathered by Barclays Bank and the Business Growth Fund that show that 49% of new businesses in 2013 were started with funding or investment of under £2,000 (roughly $3,000), and in fact 10% needed no money at all. If you do need money, there are more ways to get it than ever before, such as venture capital, a loan from a financial institution, friends and family, or even the increasingly popular crowd-funding sites like Indigogo and Kickstarter.

If you structure your ideas and marketing the right way, which I will be helping you to do in this book, raising funds at the right point of your entrepreneurial journey should be far easier, enabling you to grow the business and make it highly profitable. Don't feel you need money to start with as an entrepreneur, or that when you do need it you will have problems getting it, because that's simply no longer the case.

Talking of money, many feel that being an entrepreneur is all about making money – WRONG.

You don't have to be focused on money. Setting your sights on solving social problems, or should I say, moving the game on when it comes to social issues, sometimes delivers financial rewards at the same time, but fundamentally the rewards are different, yet equally valid to an entrepreneurial mentality. Don't be averse to making money as a social entrepreneur – don't assume social entrepreneurs can't or shouldn't make money, because when they do, they can do even more amazing things for others as a result, so it's really a double win for their cause. Many entrepreneurs who were initially financially led get involved in charitable causes too, again Richard Branson is a good example, as is Bill Gates.

People often feel that others will not support them in their decision to become an entrepreneur – WRONG.

Here in the UK, people are less dynamic and more reserved, maybe even more cautious, than they are in some other countries, and this limiting outlook may be quite real to you, especially if friends and family seem unsupportive to start with. If you want to be an entrepreneur you have to accept that you must be opinionated, and be prepared to defend your opinion at all times, so stand up for your beliefs and you will be amazed how people will actually change their opinions when they see the positive impact becoming an entrepreneur has on you.

And the last limiting belief is when people say, "I don't know what I could do or whether it will work" – IT'S EASY TO FIX THIS, so let's get on with doing that right now.

First and foremost, it's important to understand that you don't have to be first in a market, or create your own market; in fact being successful is often less likely under these conditions, because the market will question you and it will be much harder to convert your idea into a successful project or business.

However, you should be quite clear in your own mind that entrepreneurs, and therefore you, must be "future centric". You need to look ahead, not back. Things behind you are only there to learn from and use as relevant experience to shorten the time, cost and problems associated with success. The great thing is that you can use other people's history, like mine here in this book, to learn from too, supporting your future. Education and experience are not relevant, but I will say the ability to learn is, and there's a whole chapter on doing this effectively.

It should be noted that the speed and level of success you will have is based on how easy it is for those whose problem you are solving, to adopt your solution, and here's the key to everything – be a reverse engineer, not a researcher.

You may wish to look at an area of interest, like a hobby, as the starting point for your new venture, and so long as you can move the game on that's fine. However, in my experience and opinion, you should never ever just start because you enjoy something; this will almost certainly cloud or distort your perception of the market and the market's needs. Let me give you my own example here.

If I were to start a business based on my hobbies, it would involve luxury, performance or racing cars. I had car posters on my bedroom walls when I was growing up, I still read car magazines, I visit car websites, I have model cars dotted around, illustrations and paintings of cars in frames rather than posters on the walls now (but only where I'm allowed them in the house); even my office is car-themed – the chair I am sitting on as I write this book is a classic Ferrari-style chair in red and cream leather, a gift from Alison. I'm very fortunate to have some nice cars of my own to drive, and have had most of the "dream" cars in my garage at one time of another. A few years ago I started to race cars, competing at some of the iconic racetracks around the world, but I'm not telling you all this to brag, in fact I just want you to appreciate that I am a "car nut", or as we call somebody like me here in the UK, a "petrolhead"; I even own the domain name, that's how fanatical I am.

Anyway, I realise, much as I would love to have a business selling these types of car, my commercial judgement would be influenced by my passion – the fact is, I would struggle to sell them in some cases. If I had a car magazine, something that wouldn't be too difficult based on my previous experience and skills, I would be more interested in driving the cars and writing the articles, than making the business profitable, and even though every so often I have a good idea or two on how to move car-related games on, the reality is that I am better at focusing on other entrepreneurial opportunities that then allow me to buy and enjoy cars. I highly recommend you to be mindful of my little story before you think that your hobby is the right market to enter as an entrepreneur; but if you can move the game on and stay commercially objective, then you are in luck because that really is the perfect situation to be in.

The key to the right idea, or continued set of ideas, is being able to ask the right questions at the right time of yourself, your market and those you work with. You have to be careful that your current assumptions and interests aren't going to hold you back.

Often the best place to start your search for an idea is where you currently work; that way, you have some experience of what happens, and from this you can make improvements that you know the market wants but other companies are not delivering. Moving the game on doesn't have to be revolutionary; you may actually find that your idea is about a small element of a business, for example customer service, or specialisation in a particular market, so don't worry if your idea isn't a big one, so long as it adds value to your target market.

Another area to consider would be one where you are a consumer of a product or service, but are frustrated by the fact that what you want or need is not available. This may be because what you are looking for has not yet been invented or created; it may be because the price or quality of what is offered to you is not right, but equally it could just be that geographically, the item or service you want exists but is just not easily available locally.

No matter what you decide is a good opportunity for you as an entrepreneur, make sure there is demand for it. All too often I see this mistake; I too have been guilty of failing to test the market, but in the next chapter I will explain how to validate an idea and turn it into a business.

The last thing you can do is to come up with not just an idea that moves the game on, but rather a completely new game. This is very, very rare – even success stories like Amazon didn't do this, what they did was spot an opportunity, not a new market. You could argue that people like Google and Facebook did come up with a new game, but the challenge with a new game is convincing people to play. It's far easier, faster and more cost-effective to update and modify something you know has a market demand, than to create your own market.

On more than one occasion, I have tried to create a totally new "game", and each time my costs have been much higher than I anticipated, the stress levels higher too, and I have yet to turn any of them into the next billion-dollar business, even though I am still convinced they could have been, or in a couple of cases still could be. I'm not saying you shouldn't try and bring a completely new idea to market, and as an entrepreneur I know you will be passionate about it, but if this is your strategy then just be aware that it's not the easiest way to succeed, and be ready for the challenges you will face.

One example of when I tried to create a brand new market was when I had a business that developed multi-platform software that, about 10 years ago, enabled you to back-up the information on your mobile phone, even your pictures and ringtones if your phone was able to do those things (that's how long ago this was), automatically over the phone network, or if you were lucky enough to have a phone that had this function, over wi-fi . This business, called Phone Backup, was very expensive to build and I ended up building a team of sales and admin people as well as programmers, creating phone apps well before any iPhone existed. I felt that if we were able to deliver the service to just 0.25% of the market we would be highly profitable, so it seemed like a good business proposition.

The short version of the Phone Backup story is that we managed, after quite some time, to create a stable and really effective solution, but we were ahead of our time. People were concerned about things like the data costs on their phones, and even though we launched the product and ended up with thousands of customers paying us every month, the reality was we were spending significant sums of money to build a market which had not previously existed, and that was hard work, not to mention costly. Although we continued for several years and turned it into a (just) profitable business, technology overtook us as the iPhone arrived. All of a sudden, the demand for Phone Backup started to decline as our customers moved over to smartphones and their need for what we had disappeared. The moral of my story is, there's no reason not to try and invent a new game, as I call it, but it's not the easiest way to start out as an entrepreneur, as I have mentioned, and even though the rewards can be high, the risks are too, more of which I will talk about in Chapter 8.

One really great thing that I have discovered about being an entrepreneur, is that you don't have to give up on a great idea, even one for a totally new market, especially when you know or can predict the right time to "put it on ice", as I have done on several occasions in the last few years, because when you do this, all you then need to do is identify the right time and market conditions to bring it back to life, as you will see later on in the book. Alternatively what you learned and have "put on ice" can also be modified, as new opportunities present themselves, so make sure that your ideas never die because there's a great chance that additional or new value can be extracted from what you have done already at some time in the future.

The final thing to say about developing a successful idea is that it needs to have measurable benefits to your market, and measurable stages of development too, if you are to successfully convert it into a business. As an entrepreneur, you will be operating in a results-based economy where you are paid, not according to the time and effort you expend, but on the basis of your own results set against the market's expectations. Anybody who does not want to be measured or who argues against measurement is not an entrepreneur and is not likely to be successful. It may sound harsh, but it's a reality and a key part of the entrepreneurial lifestyle.

The critical things to know as we reach the end of this chapter are that you need to start with an idea that is designed to solve a problem, and if you can come up with one, a big idea for a big problem too. This doesn't mean you have to come up with the next billion-dollar business, or be a leading expert in a marketplace to be successful, you just need an idea that is big enough for your target market to take notice of, because your product or service must be relevant, distinctive and offer excellent value to your chosen market. As I have said in the past, I have yet to find a market where you can't make money as an entrepreneur, so I suggest making your life as easy as you can, at least to start with.

By the way, with the right time and guidance, it's highly likely you will be able to achieve at least 80% of your goals, however big they are – which is also the reason you should always set big, but realistic goals as an entrepreneur, if you can, because you want to move the game on, not just be a business-owner wanting to run a successful business.

CHAPTER 4

TAKING AN IDEA AND TURNING IT INTO A BUSINESS

By now, I'm sure you have realised that there's no reason why you can't be an entrepreneur, if that is what you want. But there may come a time when you are no longer entrepreneurial, and as such just become just a business-owner – this often happens to people when they reach a certain level of comfort or contentment in what they do, and are no longer looking to "move the game on", so it's vital that you make sure that you take the necessary steps, as soon as possible, to turn your idea into a business. By creating your business in the right way to start with, this also gives you the opportunity, if you want it, to continue to be an entrepreneur for as long as you want and not get bogged down or frustrated by having to run the business, because when it's a business you can find other people to operate the business, allowing you to get on with what you enjoy.

So here's the thing: creativity, determination and a bit of naivety are all essential if you are an entrepreneur, but don't play a game unless you know the principles behind what allows you to win that game, because these elements, in my experience, can create the perfect combination when you want to take a great idea and turn it into a successful business.

Business is all about replicable frameworks. I really want you to start thinking this way too; and notice I say "business is", not "being an entrepreneur is". There are too many people, whether they are business-owners or entrepreneurs, who fail to get the most basic yet important part right, and this is what will allow them to have the lifestyle they dreamed of when they first started, not the lifestyle they have now, because that's not what I want to happen to you. Let me explain.

People tend to start out with a set of goals, or some may call them dreams, and a typical dream is one where people have more money than they need, plenty of free time to enjoy themselves, and are happy. Simply put, people set out to become millionaires, or so they think, but actually they set out to have a millionaire's lifestyle, not simply that amount of money in the bank.

People never knowingly start a project with a plan based on working 14 or more hours a day, spending way more money than initially planned and working weekends as well as not taking holidays, or if they do, spending most of the holiday on the phone or email, but this is what can and does happen. I accept that to start with as an entrepreneur, you need to put in the time and effort; without it, you cannot expect to have the successful outcome you want. I say this based on my own experience; so far, I've never come up with an idea that results in me doing little or no work yet delivers large sums of money to me day in, day out; by the way if you come up with a business that does, please let me know.

Anyway enough of the sarcasm; let me tell you about a personal experience and then you can see what I did, why I did what I did, and how things are now, which I think you would like to have happen to you. As I mentioned earlier in the book, I have been involved in publishing and one particular area is magazine publishing. The first magazine title I had was related to boats; I like boats and have a place on the south coast of England, so when the opportunity arose to take over a failing magazine, I was keen. Anyway, I had my existing team of people take over production and advertising sales, working with the existing editorial team, and in a single issue, just one month, I turned a failing and unprofitable magazine into a profitable one.

Based on my past success and my other business interests, a couple of years ago I started to work on a concept I call Direct Response Publishing, and decided to put together a team of people to deliver the first magazine of its type in the world, based on the topic of women's fashion, combining direct response marketing, entertainment and shopping in one publication. I am not the most fashionable person, but my partner Alison and what we call her "fashion friends" are. Many of them work for well-known brands and fashion retailers, or as entrepreneurs in the fashion market; in fact Alison has even launched her own successful fashion collection, getting coverage in magazines like *Vogue* and *Grazia* and on TV too, so conducting the research and getting it "right" for the market was not hard, but actually quite fun and also rewarding. The basic fact was that the consumer feedback was really good; however, I wanted to get the right structure and team in place, and this is where things became harder, because other people failed to perform or to follow the framework and systems that had been put in place, which meant that the launch was delayed and my workload, instead of reducing, just got bigger and bigger. Without going into all the boring details, it's important I share with you what was relevant, and the end result; simply put, even though significant time, money and effort had been invested, I made the decision to stop working on the project as I needed to, as I put it "have a clear out".

I knew, because of my knowledge of what was possible in the industry, not just the fashion market, and the fact that what I had created had now shifted from being an idea into being a business, making things easily replicable and profitable if those who ran the business followed the "rules of the game", that by stopping and taking a moment to see what was right and what was wrong, I could make decisions and correct mistakes that were being made, before they got out of hand. I had my measurement system in place and so it was it was the best thing to do and not only that, easy to do too.

I had made sure everything I needed was in place as the idea became a business, but also things I personally didn't need (and that's a key point to remember as an entrepreneur) could be identified and could be removed; even a whole business, people and commercial partners. The result for the fashion publication, even though I am not contractually allowed to give you details, for obvious reasons, is that I now license the business model to the people who were originally working with me and who were employed by me to do the job. I have absolutely no involvement or work to do, and now all I have to do is bank the cheques when they arrive before each issue is published; I have not had to sell anything or give any of my intellectual property away, it really is passive income with zero outlay because of the work I did in advance. I can even sell the business model to others too, if I wish.

There are a few things for you to take from my fashion magazine experience, but before I highlight them I want to make sure you have a very simple example, not just my example, as this will serve you in your shift from idea to business.

I'll use the car industry as an example because, as you know, I love cars. There is a design and development process, where they innovate and "move the game on", but as soon as they can, they want to make sure they build a production line. This means that they can build many more cars, reducing the unit cost (cars built in the innovation stage are very expensive and would never be suitable for the market), besides having quality control and consistency in place, so each and every car that comes off the end of the line meets or exceeds the standards set in every area, and they can also measure productivity and profitability. And here's the most important point: on a production line, so long as you have a system that is teachable, you can add, reduce or change people and components if necessary, within the system without compromising the end result, and that's what you should be aiming for.

Systemising your idea makes it a business. Now I know better than most that entrepreneurs can be "control freaks"; I know I am one, and I have had to learn not to be, which is why I am a member of the Strategic Coach programme, something I will explain more about later. I get round this by what I have called the "McDonald's principle". I like to know how to do each process involved in my business, not just come up with ideas – even though I may not wish to do them all, or indeed any of them later on, because that's not where my time and skills are best utilised. Just as at the famous fast food chain teaches, I want to learn how to do each step of the production; that way I can contribute, understand what people need to know and not know, and also manage things better – how many times have you worked with people who seem to have no idea what it takes to do a job?

So you see, using fast food as a metaphor for turning your entrepreneurial idea into a business, you want to know how to cook the fries, flip the burgers, order the supplies, add the sauce and salad to a burger, sweep the floors, clean the tables, serve the customers, and count the money that comes in. The McDonald's principle describes the process of being able to build and continually refine a fast food production experience. That's the strategy behind a successful, profitable, replicable fast food business; it's also the core strategy behind building your own successful and profitable business.

I hate to see people walk away from understanding each step in a process because they are entrepreneurs, or think that's somebody else's job; that's just not going to serve you well. So get involved, learn what needs to be done, and make everything you can possibly make into a replicable, measurable and reliable system that does not require your day-to-day involvement, because that's the best way to continue being an entrepreneur rather than having to be a business-owner – or worse still, as I hear all too often, a slave to the business.

As a personal example, as part of my family's marketing services business, we used to have a print division. Not only was I able to identify an opportunity and make the decision to invest several hundred thousand pounds in printing equipment, making use of my entrepreneurial skill-set, but I learned how to run a printing press too. Running a printing press is no simple task, and being a print-minder is a skilled job that I never intended to do, but by learning what to do and why, I could help that side of the business much more, communicate more effectively with the print-minders and the people involved, even suppliers and customers, and on the odd occasion, I was able to help out too. I remember on more than one occasion when a person was ill, because we operated 24 hours a day, I would work through the night to literally keep the presses rolling, which if I am honest I actually quite enjoyed.

Let me just give you some more tactics that you can apply when converting an idea into a business.

I want you to know that you needn't be afraid of what you don't know, because you can find somebody who does or you can learn to do it, as I did with the printing machinery; it's also what I did with the Direct Response Publishing fashion magazine (as I say, I am not the most fashionable person; in fact my weekend attire is straight from the set of "Back to the Future", according to Alison, not off the catwalk, and my knowledge of women's fashion is even less complete).

Also learn where your skills and passion lie, and try to maximise your time on those areas, not on things you are not so good at – this strategy will deliver the best and fastest results for you. You were probably taught that if you are not good at something, then you need to work harder at it; now call me stupid if you like, but why oh why would you think spending time, effort and potentially money on something you are not good at, or maybe don't even like, is a good idea? Get somebody else to do it – you are not at school, where copying your classmate's work will get you in trouble. Smart entrepreneurs know they can't do everything, but by surrounding themselves with people who do those things exceptionally well, when these are relevant to the business, it makes light work of tasks and allows you to grow and profit faster.

Here is another revelation – or at least a good way to think: it's OK to be lazy or lethargic now and again. In fact I see this as a good thing for entrepreneurs, because it encourages you to find efficient solutions, and in fact your passion and enthusiasm will mean that when you are focused on your goals, your productivity will be far greater anyway. It's better to focus for an hour or two in a single day on what you like and are good at, rather than try and force yourself to be productive 100% of the time.

Here's another thing to realise, ideas don't make you an entrepreneur; taking action does. Action, rather than ideas, is also where the value is created. Nothing will happen unless you proactively do things to make your vision a reality. On this point I have created some more video training for you, so make sure you have signed up at **www.theentrepreneursbook.com**, because this will show you where the value in your business comes from. When you can do this, you will be almost unstoppable as an entrepreneur.

When turning your ideas into businesses, just remember you cannot control everything. You have to be aware of the market you operate in, and mindful of changes and influences that are beyond your control, as well as potential threats to your entrepreneurial journey, just like I had to be with my Phone Backup business when smartphones arrived and people no longer needed my service. It wasn't that the service was no good, it was just that the game had moved on, and because I was able to spot this I was able to make the relevant changes at the right time, maximising the income and minimising costs and ultimately potential losses.

If you are looking for customers then you are doing the wrong thing. You should always be looking to help people move from where they are now to where they want to be – this is what should shape and influence your product or service design and development, as well as all your promotional activity. This will result in better, more profitable and loyal customers. More on this later in Chapter 9.

Finally in this chapter, now that I have shared my fashion magazine story with you, I just want to remind you that as an entrepreneur, there are only two reasons for you to do something if you recall: first, because you want to, or secondly, because somebody is paying you to. The best reason of all is to have people paying you to do something you want to do.

In summary, remember you can't and don't need to do everything yourself. As an entrepreneur, your goal is to turn your ideas into a system that anybody, with the right training and equipment and facilities, can do, allowing you to keep moving the game on. Finally, if you don't know how to do something, if you are not very good at it or don't like doing it, get somebody else to do it. Those are the ways to take an idea and turn it into a business.

CHAPTER 5

HOW TO MAKE MONEY AND HOW TO LOSE MONEY TOO

For most entrepreneurs, making money, if not the primary goal, is one of them. I completely understand this – I like making money too. And don't underestimate this as a goal, because making money is not always easy. But one thing I have also learned is how to lose money, which is not something I would normally shout about, but in this case it's really helpful to you. You will find that whenever you lose money, the lesson learned is much more memorable and so, because I don't want you to lose money, I'm going to tell you how this happens too so you can avoid the mistakes I made.

A question I get all the time from fellow entrepreneurs and business-owners is "How much should I charge?" Obviously I'm not working directly with you, so I can't give you an exact figure, or for that matter an estimate, but I can help you determine that figure. Pricing is the number one factor when it comes to making, and for that matter losing, money, so not doing my best to give you a straight answer would be letting you down. That's never my intention, so here goes.

Deciding on a price is all about being able to value the solution to a problem, and here's something that is key. If you have a product or service that faces direct competition, it will be treated as a commodity, and therefore price will become a major issue. I will talk much more about this important point later on. As an entrepreneur, your focus and strategy is geared to moving the game on and solving customer problems. A really beneficial side-effect of doing this is that you can put a value on a problem – or at the very least, estimate the value of the problem. Let me give you an example.

Let's imagine that you have discovered that 10% of people who have an iPhone break their screen, and you have come up with an idea and developed a way to stop this happening. The cost of iPhone screen repair varies, but if you take your phone to Apple they just replace the phone at a cost of about £130, if I recall correctly (and yes, before you ask, I have dropped my iPhone and broken the glass). Anyway, back to the pricing methodology: I must ask, "What would somebody pay, almost like an insurance policy, not to have this problem?" I always suggest that if you can profitably sell the solution to the end-user (and that point is critical, so we will cover it in a moment, as you may end up not selling direct to the end-user) for between 5 and 10% of the value of the problem, then that is a good guide. So in this case, my iPhone screen breakage prevention system could sell for between £6.50 and £13.00 and I would suggest that at a retail price point of £9.99 it would sell very well.

I mentioned about selling to the end-user a moment ago, and it may be that you actually sell to retailers or even wholesalers, so you have to think about this too. As a guide, if you are selling to a retailer or wholesaler, you need to sell at a price around 40 to 65% below the retail price – maybe more, but obviously this depends on the market, the volumes you are selling to them, and many other factors, but we'll take that figure as a guide. By the way, I'm sure you don't need me to say this (but I will say it anyway): the calculations for selling a car are very different from selling clothes or stationery, so get to know what's right for your chosen market before you start making products to sell.

But you are probably asking, "What if I'm offering a service or something that is not a product-based idea?" Then again, look at the value the market will place on what you are providing and make what you offer not just compelling as a service, but price-wise too. Let me give you another example.

Let's imagine you have created what people call an information product, this could be an online training course, something I have done several times. When it comes to pricing, I always start by asking, "If people follow exactly what you tell them to do, and they have a good product or service, what difference will what you have make to them?" For example, if you know that by learning and applying what you teach, they will be able to make £100,000, charging them a small percentage, for example 1% of that amount is fine, so here's a simple example of just that. If I met you in the street and said to you, "If you give me £1,000 I will spend the next couple of hours with you, and after that time with me, in the next week, with no money, you could make £100,000", is that a good offer at a good price? I think so. It would be a good deal at 10 times the price, if my offer is guaranteed, so yes it is a good deal; by the way, I will show you how to pitch your idea and business and also about guarantees later on, so don't worry.

I like to make sure that I have plenty of margin in my entrepreneurial ideas, because this give me a bit more freedom to invest in them and also the marketing of them. It's worth me telling you now that, more often than not, it's not the best product that sells more and makes the most money, it's the best marketing that does, so having the money to invest on marketing, advertising and PR is critical; this element is often under-funded by inexperienced entrepreneurs. To that end, you should never be afraid of selling a high-priced product, if you see the market demand for it. In fact, sometimes this is a great strategy. Most people automatically assume a higher price means that it's a better product or service, and there is a certain section of any market who will want to buy the best and most expensive item; just make sure you are actually selling something that this segment of a market will appreciate, and you should do very well. Remember, they want value too, just in a different way.

I also like to make sure I don't have to discount, unless I want to shift old stock or increase my sales volumes, but I always try to avoid selling at anything less than a healthy profit. As you are probably aware, there are certain markets where discounting is an everyday occurrence. Just think about the last time you saw an advert on TV for a home furnishings store in your area and they didn't have a sale – not easy, is it? But here's something worth thinking about, IKEA are probably the world's most successful furniture retailer and they only have a sale occasionally, not every day, because they price their products and educate their potential customers correctly in the first place. You need to do the same. If you do have a sale or offer discount, do it on your terms to shift stock that is about to be surplus to requirement, and on that note, try and make sure you don't have, if possible, any unsaleable or hard-to-sell stock. If you do, turn it into cash as fast as you can, even if you have to sell it at a loss; this way you can use that cash to buy something new that will make you money.

Like most entrepreneurs, I have been guilty of not following my own advice in the past. I recall the time about six or seven years ago, maybe more, when I was offering a service that used Bluetooth to transmit sales and marketing messages in places like shopping and exhibition centres. It was starting to go well and the business was beginning to build a good Bluetooth network and a good reputation too. The service was in many prime locations across the UK, but the mistake was the sales team started to let customers negotiate too much. Experience tells me that sales people tend to focus on sales and revenue, not profit, and with the Bluetooth marketing service, customers negotiated hard and were trying to dictate how much they would pay to access the system and send messages. The reality was they did not pay a sufficient amount, and the fees didn't allow the business to operate profitably in the medium term because there was no money for continued investment. In the short term this was fine, but you should never go to a market without at least a medium-term view of how it will develop. The result of this failure to maintain the price was that we had to stop offering Bluetooth marketing, because I did not want to affect the profitability of other parts of that business, which can happen if you don't identify potential issues fast.

I see that the same basic principles behind what I did with Bluetooth are back with Apple's iBeacon project and I can see what the market opportunity has to offer an entrepreneur, but equally, I see the potential pitfalls and know the mistakes I made in the past. Suffice to say, if I do get involved in this area, which I've been asked about on a consultancy basis for a company who are interested in taking Apple's iBeacon concept to market, I will be very clear as to what I will do, based on the investment required for a medium to long-term business opportunity, so this is why I highly recommend using my own and other's experience as a great way to make money and avoid losing money too.

One thing people often fail to appreciate is that not everybody is going to buy in to what you are offering them – even if they should (back to my iPhone example, everybody should protect their screen with a £9.99 item), but I always base my expectations on managing to secure no more that about 2%, or at most 5%, of a given market. I regularly sit down with people who are setting out on their entrepreneurial journey, and start with some simple questions. I suggest you ask yourself:

- Who is going to pay me for my product or service?

- How much will they pay me?

- What profit is there?

And here's the big one that I think too many people fail to ask…

- How much do I want to earn?

The reason for the last question is simple: I want people to reverse-engineer everything they can in their idea development, and most importantly their business, from this crucial figure. Let's use a simple example and I will show you what I mean. I have also created a video and a really fun exercise for you in the members' area of **www.theentrepreneursbook.com**, because I want you to expend energy in the right areas as fast as possible, and not waste your skills as an entrepreneur.

Let's imagine you want to earn £100,000 a year. Your product or service idea sells for £200 per time. Now at this point many people, especially those who offer online courses, tend to say that you need sell only 500 units; that would make £100,000 revenue, but your business has operating costs, even if these are very low. Being more realistic, from the sale of £200 you may, for example, have a profit margin of 25%, so £50, after all your production, management, admin, marketing and taxation costs, so the reality is that to make your £100,000 a year you need to sell 2,000 units.

If this was the situation you faced, next I would want you to ask yourself – because you need to sell 2,000 a year, and that's quite a few – first of all, is that a realistic sales target? A good tip is to split these 2,000 sales into a daily sales amount, so in this case, based on selling 365 days a year, can you sell five and a half items per day? If the answer is yes, then great. The second question is, depending upon the market, can you increase the price, reduce costs or hopefully both? Can you turn the £50 profit per item into £80? Because by doing this it means you then only have to sell 3.5 a day, which is much easier. Now you can see why in some industries, they say that you make money when you buy an item of your stock, not when you sell it, and also why a business has to be clear that every £1 it spends has to be an investment and be able to help you make a profit or, because you are an entrepreneur, improve your lifestyle.

The moral here is, be clear on what you want at the outset, especially on your personal income side, as this may be relevant to your personal circumstances, and it should definitely influence the ideas you work on. It's as important to know what you don't want as it is to know what you do want, as both have equal relevance in becoming successful and should be at the heart of you being an entrepreneur.

The next thing to note is that you shouldn't waste time, money or effort on those people who are not potential customers. In most cases, this is the biggest mistake people make, and as such I advise you to have a system that automatically sorts prospects out, something that I will share more about later on in the book. It's worth knowing that people don't buy for one of only three reasons: they don't want it, they can't afford it, or you haven't convinced them that you are the person to provide it. This latter reason can be complex, more on this later. I see many people, especially sales people, fail to understand this fully and it's potentially the fastest way to lose money.

Another loss-making activity that almost every business suffers from is not realising that, just because somebody is not ready to buy in to what you offer straight away, doesn't mean that you should forget about him or her. As many as 80% of your potential customers are not ready to buy now, or in the next seven days. But you want, in fact need, to be there when they *are* ready to buy – again, something I will cover in more detail later.

It's my view that the best way for you to make money is to be proactive, rather than reactive, in as many situations as possible. I would like to be proactive in all situations but that's not realistic; however, you can get quite close if you put your mind to it. You need to look out for the threats as well as the opportunities in business, because moving the game on requires you to do both – just ask former employees of companies like Blockbuster, Borders Books and other well-known business casualties about what happens when you are not proactive about the threats.

The same skills you use for spotting the ways to move the game on will also protect you; in my case, I read many things, listen to podcasts, keep an eye on certain websites, buy trade publications not just from the UK but from overseas too and, as a general rule, I keep my eyes open to as many things as I can, because being an entrepreneur is not, I would say, a 9 to 5, Monday to Friday activity – it's my personality. Another thing I do is actually task people in my businesses to, every day, as their first job, check and report on certain things in the marketplaces where I operate. They are doing the initial research, and as such I can identify what I need to apply myself to faster and more efficiently, whether that's competitor prices or their marketing and advertising messages. I even want to know what's trending and popular on iTunes and on certain websites; early identification of things is a key skill entrepreneurs should develop (and I actually find it quite fun, too).

Next, I want to highlight something that some people may find quite controversial, but in my opinion one of the biggest mistakes people can make is to work according to accepted business or accounting principles, for example a balance sheet. As an entrepreneur, I see that money is different now, not just in its value – £100 today, based on inflation over the last 40-odd years, is the equivalent of only £9.50 in 1973, yet certain items have changed in value by very different amounts, so that after that same period, beer costs almost 20 times more, a house is 18 times more expensive, petrol and diesel costs 17 times more to buy, and gold is 30 times more valuable. So the value of money changes and it also depends on taxation, which is not a good thing for an entrepreneur, as it can make an item overpriced if you are not careful. Knowing and predicting the value of money in your market can help you decide where you should trade, both in terms of market sector and even geographically: just look at the gambling industry, where people are trading from tax-efficient locations. If you can see where the value of an item, skill or market will outperform an alternative location, or how you can gain a competitive and profit advantage, this is a good way to ply your entrepreneurial skills.

Money is often seen as a measurement and a way to keep score, almost like a game, but it has to be understood in context, especially when credit is far easier to access than before, and there are new ways to pay, like Bitcoins, and many other factors to consider. Things we traditionally thought of as constants in our economy are changing; so be open to new and alternative financial concepts, even if they challenge long-standing beliefs. That way you will not suffer because of potential limiting beliefs.

I also recommend that you stop using a balance sheet as anything other than a "snapshot" of your business's situation. As an entrepreneur, you should be looking at sales, expenses and, at the end of the day, week or month, the cash you have to spend in whatever way you want; this is part of the freedom you get as an entrepreneur, rather than just as a business-owner or employee, and you can change things too if you want more money to spend, or wish to trade money for another benefit such as time, or a reduction in stress, because you can do this too. If you don't have the money to spend on what you want to spend it on, it's not really a profit in my eyes, even if an accountant says it is, so when you want to know how to make money, think about spending it, which is something you will see in the video I mentioned earlier on in this chapter; it's a fun exercise to do too.

What about some more specific tactics you can use to make money? Well, I always think you need to make sure you have an integrated suite of products and services, not a single one, even if it takes time to make them all work in harmony; just think about how Apple have become so successful and powerful. They have the computer, the phone, the tablet, the online store to buy software, the platform that allows customers not only to manage but also buy music, movies, books and much more. They even have physical retail outlets too.

Another perfect example of the integrated product suite, in a very different industry to Apple, is IKEA. If you have ever been in one of their stores, you will know that what they call their "marketplace" has all sorts of accessories and associated products that people seem to buy in vast quantities. It's a perfectly designed and executed integrated strategy that all we entrepreneurs can learn from, model and apply in our own businesses.

I do my best to make sure that everybody who works for and with me understands that his or her job is making the company money – it's not just based on a simple job description. I love the fact that companies like Zappos want everybody to try and come up with a way, each and every day, to improve what they do and what the company can do for their customers by 1%. Just think of improvement in this way – making a 1% improvement is quite easy and it can come from virtually any and every part of a business, but that improvement has a compound effect, and at the end of just a week, think of the impact all that improvement has – it's way beyond 7%. That's something I will talk more about when it comes to harnessing technology as an entrepreneur, later on in the book.

On what I suppose you can a describe as a collaborative approach to making money, remember I mentioned a moment ago, "everybody who works for and with me…". Well I like to make sure that suppliers are treated well – something that I know Zappos believe too. I always try to pay a fair price for a job, not as they say here in the UK "screw" every last penny out of a deal. If you have great suppliers who you are fair with, who you trust and who, in return, trust you too, your whole approach to being in business can become a win-win relationship, and less stressful too. That, to me, is a key point when it comes to making money. Be honest and fair with customers, staff and suppliers, and you give yourself the best possible chance of long-term success.

Here in the UK, in my opinion, too many people seem to think it's OK if a supplier doesn't make money – or if they do, it should be a minimal amount, and they should be happy to be a supplier. I think it should be the other way round and if you do too, then that sets you up to deliver great service and value for your customers, not just for your suppliers.

There are some well-known businesses that are proud of their aggressive attitude and treatment of suppliers, that actually set up their structure to minimise supplier-customer relationships and that, on a financial and personal level, deliberately treat suppliers badly. Personally I have been on the receiving end of this. In one particular instance I remember having a meeting with a big UK retailer about the Phone Backup service I mentioned earlier. I went to this meeting because the sales guy wanted my support, as it was potentially a big deal. We were deliberately left in reception for almost 90 minutes after the time when the meeting was meant to start; it wasn't until I said to reception that I had other things to do and was leaving that the person I was having the meeting with decided to come down to meet us. You can imagine the atmosphere in that meeting, and my propensity to want to do business with them. This particular experience was definitely a learning experience, and maybe that's why now I only do things I want to do or that people are paying me to do: a rule that continues to serve me well; in fact it saves me, on average, over 12 hours a week in travel and meeting time, and also makes what I do more profitable, so, as they say, "every cloud has a silver lining". By the way, I hear from other people I know in various industries, that this company often do this type of thing and call suppliers in to meetings at anti-social times, just for effect, so look out for it if you ever have to deal with this type of organisation and only do it if you want to.

While I'm on the subject of big companies, the days when big companies were in control of the market have almost vanished now. Recent sales and valuations like WhatsApp or AirBnB show that with a small entrepreneurial team you don't need to be a big company to be worth billions, so another great way to make money (and avoid losing money too) is to stay small, lean and agile. Big companies have big problems, and often only survive because of the momentum they have in a marketplace, but very few big companies are naturally entrepreneurial. In fact they like to acquire entrepreneurial companies as a way to grow their own business and to be seen as innovators and dynamic, but the reality is this is a great opportunity for you and it's what large entrepreneurial companies do, just like Google, who have a whole department called "X" dedicated to moving the game on without the need to perform or conform to the way the business runs day-to-day.

So as you can see, managed entrepreneurial behaviour, not just watching the costs of buying and selling, is the key to success. The simple matter of keeping costs as low as possible, and prices right for your market, is one thing, but that's probably not too exciting. But as an entrepreneur the fact that you can apply logic to your game-changing ideas and profit from this is a major attraction, no matter what industry or marketplace you are changing for the better.

Making money is not easy – if it was, everybody would be doing it, but the principles behind it can be expressed quite simply:

There are only three ways to make more money, once you have a great product or service that people want to buy, and these are, first, to get more customers; we will cover this later on.

Second is to sell each customer more things, sometimes called increasing average basket value. This is all part of the idea behind an integrated product suite, and why companies like Amazon are keen to show you additional products you might like to buy, at the click of a single button, that up the sale amount.

Third is get people to buy more frequently from you. This too can be done with an integrated product suite, and also by designing a product or service to achieve this, so remember this when you are brainstorming ideas, because as an entrepreneur, this is where you can really win in comparison to being just a business-owner.

And one final tip, when it comes to making money. It's something Jimmy, my wire-haired dachshund can teach you – yes, that's right, rather than teaching an old dog a new tricks (except he's not that old), he can teach you one, and it's this: when you want something and you know it's there, focus on the goal, focus on the person or people who can give it to you, and nothing else. Make that person or people aware that you are there and that you want it. Don't be subtle about it either, change tactics if you feel you are not getting noticed or if you are not moving closer to your goal, even if it takes time and effort, and even if you have to learn a new skill. As Jimmy would tell you, if he could talk: never give up, because eventually you will get what you want. And if he can do it, what's stopping you?

CHAPTER 6
THE SHORT CUTS TO SUCCESS

We all like a short cut, especially when it's a short cut to success. I want you to have the key to finding as many short cuts to success as you could ever want; I will also tell you what I do and why.

The way to get from where you are now to where you want to be in the least time, with the least effort and with the lowest cost, is to learn from others, but what I'm going to share with you has a twist.

If you merely model or copy what others are doing, then you shouldn't expect to be really successful; at best, you may be moderately successful for a short period of time. The reason I say this is that anybody else can do the same thing too, and that will mean you will not have at least one differentiating factor in your market for a prolonged period of time. Simply put, you will not have moved the game on; all you are doing is the same as somebody else.

Modelling successful people and companies can be a great way to shorten learning time and reduce risk, as well as lessening the chance of making mistakes, but that is not how to succeed – it's the way to become a commodity. When I come up with an idea, I do whatever I can to protect it, to give myself the longest possible time to exploit the opportunity; but with technology and the cost of technology, this is more difficult than ever to do. My advice is to learn from others not just in your own chosen market but from other markets too. Let me explain my logic here.

There are very few if any entirely new ideas; but equally there are very few people who proactively look for ideas and learn new things every single week, making themselves better at what they do by design, rather than by accident. You must always set aside time to improve your own abilities, whether that's by learning new skills, watching and listening to experts on a relevant subject or even using trial and error. As soon as you stop improving, you stop being an entrepreneur, as it's a key component of "moving the game on".

I have an open mind, as much as I can, and I encourage you to have an open mind too. Look to other forms of inspiration in as many relevant areas as you can, as often solutions and opportunities come from being aware of things around you, or that you find when actively searching for things that could help you. To take note of inspirational items, I use services like Evernote and Ember on my Mac, to collect things I find online or from photos I take of things that interest and inspire me. I have a filing cabinet and large cupboard in my office full of ideas, because physical items are highly relevant, whether it's a piece of direct mail or actual products I see in stores; if something is inspiring, I file it away for later.

Let me just ask you, would you prefer to be treated by a doctor who is up-to-date, knows what's possible now because of the new innovations in medicine, or somebody who hasn't done any further training and self-improvement since they left medical school? I suspect you would want the best medical care on offer from the up-to-date practitioner. Use this same logic in your area of expertise, as this is a key differentiating factor for you as an entrepreneur vs. your competition, and it also fits in with the concept of the simple diagram I first showed you in Chapter 3:

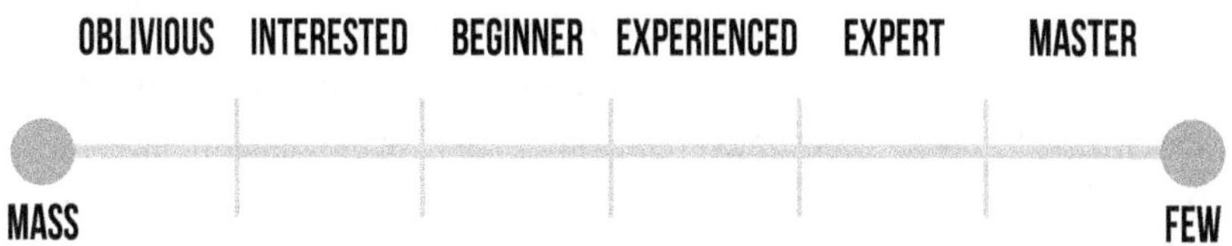

The same is true when it comes to investing in physical things you own or use. It's generally considered prudent to keep your car and home in a good state of repair; if you don't, then at some point you may have big problems, and the same is true of your business. To keep your business running effectively you need to keep things as they should be, and as an entrepreneur you want to make things better. The fastest and most reliable way to do this is by learning. The other thing to say is that education is not always like school or university. When you are an entrepreneur it's fun, inspiring, and once you have found the media formats and people you like to learn from, as I have, you will find you actually look forward to learning. I never looked forward to sitting in a classroom for hours a day, or taking exams at school or university, but I can assure you I love to improve my abilities across all sorts of business and entrepreneurial subjects now, and I expect you will too.

I always think that the best way to improve is to build up your knowledge and skill "layer by layer", as this gives you the most solid and replicable results, both now and in the future. I set aside about eight hours a week, more if I can, to listen to podcasts like iLoveMarketing.com and audiobooks, as this for me is the fastest way to integrate continual personal and entrepreneurial improvement into my week. The easy way I found to do this amount of learning was to remove the TV from the kitchen and then listen to things using an iPod docking station while eating meals or doing things around my home. I also listen to podcasts and audiobooks in the car. If you just make a few small changes, as I have, you will find that it's actually quite easy to listen to eight or more hours of educational material a week and it's a surefire way to take on new ideas and learn skills that will help you make money too.

I also invest money in my education. I am a member of a programme called Strategic Coach, and the point of this is to make sure I am learning as much as I can so I can do as good a job as possible for my businesses and customers. I find it amazing that most people – at a guess, I would say over 90% of people – do not invest any time, money or effort in becoming better at what they do for a living. Of course there are some professions where constant improvement and learning the latest, most effective solutions is a prerequisite, for example in medicine, but in general, business people seem to think they can learn on the job, or that structured education should stop after school, college or university. This is wrong on many levels, especially when constant learning and development is a short cut to success, but they are not entrepreneurs like you and I and that's why we have such a great opportunity to achieve what we want.

I'm an avid buyer and consumer of online courses; in fact these account for a significant part of the £1,500 to £2,000 a month that I invest on my education, as well as about 20% of what most people would call my working hours, over and above the eight hours of listening to podcasts and audiobooks. That may seem a lot, and the cost of this has to be factored in to what I do and how I make money, but the reality is that my investment in learning means I can get to where I want to go faster and with less waste than almost everybody else I know in my marketplaces.

Just in terms of how I bill for what I do, because I work in what I called earlier, the result economy, I am not paid per hour (if I was, I guess I would be charging about £500 an hour at the very least), but here's the thing: because results are what matter, not an hourly rate, I can do in an hour what others will take maybe four or even as many as 20 hours to achieve, if they can achieve what I can at all. The people who work with and for me can do more than most in an hour too, so I offer my customers incredible value on a results basis, but maybe not so much if you just looked at it as an hourly rate; however I hope you start to work and buy this way too, because that's how you should operate as an entrepreneur.

People do actually ask how to come up with an hourly rate if that's how they have to charge in their marketplace, and much as I would rather you didn't work this way, I want to help you with that. The reality is that even if you are the most efficient and focused person at work, one-third or more of your time will be spent making sure you are organised and learning new things, and another third will be spent on other things you can't charge for, even sales and marketing, so doing some simple maths again, if we go back to the earlier example where you want to earn £100,000 a year and you work, on average, 60 hours a week, because that's what a motivated and passionate entrepreneur is often doing (that may not be right, but it's the reality), and also you take four weeks of holiday a year, it looks like this:

60 hours per week of which 20 are billable

You work 48 weeks a year

So in total you have 20 hours x 48 = 960 billable hours

This means you have to bill more than £104 an hour to reach your £100,000 target. Now obviously this is an over-simplified example, and there are many other costs incurred when you work, but it shows you have to put a reasonable value on an hour of your time; not only that, you need to focus on the productive billable hours you have too and also the value you can generate for your customers in an hour. Anyway, back to the short cuts.

I am fortunate that I can invest money in my education because money, in this situation, is a substitute for time and exposure to risk. It will never get results on its own, but I see every pound spent as an investment, not a cost, and that's the best way to think about it in my opinion. It also helps my mind stay agile and prevents procrastination. If you are not fortunate enough to have the money to spend as I do, then podcasts are perfect, as the value they deliver is amazing and most of them are free. The right books are great value too, I am just not somebody who enjoys reading so I listen to them, as I mentioned earlier.

Websites are great as a learning tool, because people write great articles on blogs. With my own blog I try to give away as much free valuable content as I can, to help budding entrepreneurs and business-owners who don't have the ability to invest in working with me personally; in fact this book is also a way to help more people who have a limited budget, as well as those who maybe have the money to spend but want value too. In fact I want you to get much more value from the book than the price you paid for it.

Just to summarise, learn to improve what you do, and rather than model and copy what others do, learn and use it as entrepreneurial inspiration in your chosen marketplace. This way you can keep an eye on what's happening, learn from the experience of others, avoid mistakes and take the short cuts that are there and open for you all day, every day. Why make success harder than it needs to be?

CHAPTER 7

LEARN TO FAIL: DO IT OFTEN, AND AS QUICKLY AS POSSIBLE

I want to start off by saying that I hope you never make a mistake or fail, but the reality is that you will – even if only in a small way. There's a simple reason for this: as an entrepreneur you will be pushing the limits of your chosen market, and therefore you will not always get the results you planned for, so you must be able to identify the results, act on them and move on from any setbacks. And by the way, setbacks can also occur because things are too successful: you need to manage success and resources – this is an area people often struggle with, but you don't have to.

The first thing I like to do is validate a market; there are various ways to do this, but the easy and free way is to do some research online. You can use Google to search out relevant terms that relate to what you are doing, but the best way, in my experience, at least at the outset, is to get involved in online forums and see what people are asking or needing. The trick to forums and groups, no matter what platform they use, is to start by not just joining, but by adding value to the group by posting helpful information and also answering members' questions if you can. That way, when you want something, people will know who you are, that you are a positive and helpful person and that you are trusted in the group.

You can also ask questions in the form of surveys with free services like SurveyMonkey.com, but be very careful when framing the questions, so that you get the feedback you need, not the answers you want – a mistake people often make, as well as a tactic people sometimes use when they want to use the results to sell something like advertising. To me, this is wrong; as an entrepreneur it will not serve you well, and increases risks unnecessarily. Cold hard honest answers are what you need.

You can ask friends and family what they think of your ideas, or better still ask your target market if they would buy what you are planning to offer; this way you may find out if you are likely to fail beforehand – this is a fast and safe way to fail. A step on from this tactic is to actually ask people to buy what you are planning to create in advance; you will find that people are much more honest when they have to part with money. The worst-case scenario is that you find out nobody wants to buy in to your idea; at best, you make sales before you have even turned it into a business, so to me, this is a win-win strategy.

As an entrepreneur I am always wanting to do things, try things and get a reaction, so I'm always spending a little time, money and effort on marketing, advertising and PR, to see what works and what doesn't. The core of what I do and have done for over 20 years is marketing. I could write many books on the subject, but to keep things simple, as this is not a marketing book, when it comes to promotions and sales, I highly recommend that you use a technique called direct response marketing. At its heart, direct response marketing is highly measurable and can be use in print as well as in digital channels.

The basic principle behind direct response marketing is that you communicate directly with the customer using a strategy that enables you to monitor and report on results, and therefore measure your return on investment very accurately. I always say to people that setting up a marketing, advertising or PR budget is naive; what you need to do is work out a system that you know for certain delivers the results, not agree a budget. I sometimes speak at marketing and business exhibitions and events, and I often have a visual example of why I say this, which always goes down well with the audience but often not so well with other speakers who are from advertising, marketing and PR agencies, but that's their problem. Let me explain what I do and then you can, I hope, learn to use this tactic to find out what works, what doesn't and, if you are going to fail with a marketing, advertising, PR or sales strategy, you can do it fast.

When I am talking about strategy as an entrepreneur and a marketer, I say to the audience, "Is there somebody who has a £1 coin I could have?" At this point people wonder what I'm doing, but a few people reach into their pocket or bag and say yes, here you are. At this point, as they hand me the £1 coin, I then give them back a £5 or £10 note. This all depends on what I have in my wallet at the time, and say "Here you are, thank you." As you may imagine, this seems a little strange, but I then go on to explain that everything you do in business, especially marketing, needs to be an investment, and your job when spending money is to work out, fast, what profit, not just return, you get on every £1 you spend. This needs to be based on facts, not what an agency or media-owner tells you. I then go on to say, "If every time you gave me a £1 coin I gave you back a £5 or £10 note, how many £1 coins would you give me?" and the answer is always, as many as I can, and that's right, so having a limited budget actually doesn't help you; all it does is protect you from spending too much on failures, when actually you should be working out what makes you money and then doing it as much as you can or want to do.

The great thing about marketing, advertising and PR now is that you can initially limit your spending and, even in print, with the right strategies, not just with online advertising, you can measure results in an instant and work out what works and what doesn't, for less than £100 online and maybe £250 in print. The basic principle behind finding out what works is to put in place a system that takes an initial enquiry or sale and automates as much as possible, or at the very least, notes what has happened so you can learn from it.

Too many people do what is known as image advertising, and spend money on what they think is branding, things like a fancy logo, trendy graphics and websites, stylish photography and lots of things that cost money and that design professionals encourage you to do. The reality is this: after you've worked out what you should be spending your money on and what you shouldn't, the steps I'm about to share with you are what your advertising, marketing, PR or any other type of promotion must do, even trade shows. You must also do these steps in the right order too:

First, you need to show people clearly, not subtly or by trying to be clever, what you have to offer them, whether that's a product or service.

Next you want to be clear in telling them what it will do for them when the buy it; never assume they will not be buying and using it.

And finally, tell them what you want them to do next, or as some people describe this, give them a "Call to Action".

Now, because of what I do and have done over the last 20 or so years, I could write a book for each of these elements; and not only that, a book for how to do each of these with digital and traditional media outlets too, so it's quite a challenge to give you the simple answer to the next question I'm asked all the time, which is "But what sort of marketing, advertising or PR should I do?" Here's the best answer I can give you, as I am not working directly with you:

You should first advertise using social media, and in particular on Facebook, because you can really limit your expenditure and try things, learn to fail, fail often and quickly too, in fact after a bit of practice, in less than eight hours and for under £50, so it's a great investment and worth doing even before you have something to sell, just as a form of market research.

Once you know what gets positive results using something like Facebook, I suggest you look at how you can create a simple website using one of the many free or low-cost website-building systems offered by many of the domain name providers like GoDaddy, 1 & 1, or in the UK 123-Reg and other companies like Wix, SquareSpace or Moonfruit. Just do a search in Google and you will find plenty to choose from. (By the way, I have no affiliation nor do I make money by recommending any of these services in the book, I just want to help you do things efficiently and cost effectively, so you can invest in things that make money.)

If you want to take things a little further with your website, then using a platform like Wordpress is a great idea. You can buy amazing looking design templates and online functionality like online shopping carts quite cheaply. The best place to look for these, in my experience, is Themeforest.net. Many Wordpress themes automatically work across computers, laptops, tablet devices and smartphones. People access information on all sorts of devices now and you MUST, I'm going to say this again, you MUST have a website, even if it's very basic, that works across all devices, otherwise you are wasting opportunities all day, every day and that's not a mistake entrepreneurs should make.

One last thing when it comes to a website; you have to do the following, as a minimum. First of all, you need to have a website that tells people what you have and also what it will do for them; you need to let people know how they can contact you; but the two most important things are that it must capture leads (the best way to do this is with a contact form), and secondly it must add value to anybody visiting the site. I will talk about adding value to a potential customer in a couple of chapters' time. Finally, if you can, it's a great idea to make sure people can spend money on your website: if your product or service could possibly be sold this way, sell it this way.

What about traditional forms of advertising and marketing? Well I love print and I know, when it's done right, it's very, very effective as a marketing communication channel. However, based on the fact that it will cost you more than working just in the digital areas, my advice would be to first find out what works, minimising your waste in print media. The same holds true for PR: this is often expensive and not always very effective. Remember, you must measure on the basis of pure fact, not subjective opinion, what is making you money.

If you are going to use print for advertising and marketing, then I think you should make sure, as quickly as you can, that you have some good quality, nicely designed business cards. I also think direct mail, to the right prospect list (that's the key here), is fantastic value for money. I personally use all media formats for marketing, and across my business interests produce over £1,000,000 of printed marketing material a year. Print isn't necessarily far greater an expense than digital marketing, but you have to learn how best to spend your money and that's why I want you to fail, and fail fast, in order to learn how to do it right, in so much as you measure real results, not take a guess.

There are some other important things I would like to share about failing. First of all the term failure has such a negative association, so often it's better to think in terms of results. No matter what you do, you will get a result – it may not be the one you want, but you will always get a result. If you want to change the result you get, you have to change the inputs that got you that result, simple but true. Time and time again, I see people continuing to do the same things in business, marketing, and even with their entrepreneurial ideas, and wondering why they are not getting better results, and it's simple: they have not made the right changes.

If it comes to it, you must also not be afraid, at the right moment, to cut your losses and move on, as I did with the fashion magazine project I mentioned earlier. By taking action you can change the outcome, and that's a perfect example of making a hard decision but actually profiting as a result, whereas if I hadn't made the change I would still be working in a way and at a cost that I would be unhappy with, and spending money without the desired return on investment. You will find that by learning to fail correctly, as I have shared with you in this chapter, your ability to make decisions fast and stick with them will improve, which is another good reason to learn how to fail.

Once you get to a point where you can get positive and consistent results in what you do, I recommend that you make small changes across your whole business and your ideas too, because there will always be things that you can improve, again maybe by as little as just 1% each time, but added together you will find that 20% of what you do makes you 80% of your profit. This also allows your to focus on being an entrepreneur and not on other activities that you enjoy less and don't make you the money or deliver the satisfaction you desire.

There you have my logic and tactics behind failure as a way for you to actually reach, or at the very least, move closer to, your ultimate goals. In summary then, I move towards goals, and you can do this too, by continually validating, measuring and modifying what I am doing and what the resulting outcomes are, so that I am always heading, overall, in the right direction. Being an entrepreneur is a journey, and on any journey you have to know where you are at all times, to achieve your goals as quickly and efficiently as possible. Make sure to learn, and use what happens as a way to help move you towards your goals. When this happens your confidence and results will continually improve, maybe even exponentially.

CHAPTER 8

NOW IS YOUR TIME

Being an entrepreneur will never be easy, even if you do make a fortune. Accept this, but use it as a way to energise and challenge yourself day-in, day-out because that's all part of the mentality of an entrepreneur. Based on the fact that you are at this point in the book, there is every possibility that you are among the select group of people taking action and becoming a better entrepreneur. If so, I have some great news for you: now really is your time, because never before in history have the opportunities been as big for those that take action. In this chapter I'm going to explain not just why this is, but how to harness the opportunities.

By now you should be starting to appreciate that you need to be committed to what you are doing, and be strong of mind too, as those you come into contact with may not always agree with you, your ideas and your passion. However, they can only help you to take decisions, not determine what you do or don't do. The scale of technology we have access to today, especially via the Internet, is a major resource for entrepreneurs and your ally, on so many levels. When you use it correctly, you can achieve almost anything and overcome problems and obstacles because it allows you to replace external resources with your own resourcefulness, and that can be incredibly powerful.

The Internet has been around for quite some time now. I look back to when I was 17 years old and first started using it– back then you accessed information via a numerical web address, or through an aggregation service like CompuServe, and you needed a plan and some time to spare before you started even going online to find things. You couldn't ask Google, there were no social media sites and there were definitely not the types of things online I am about to talk about now and encourage you to harness as an entrepreneur.

The first reason why "now is your time" is that sites like eLance, Freelancer, CrowdFlower, 99 Designs and Tongal exist, allowing you to leverage crowds and to have a virtually unlimited resource of manpower and skills at a moment's notice.

Only a few years ago, the requirement to have in-house or relatively inflexible staff resources for business precluded many entrepreneurs from entering a market, even if they did have an amazing idea; but today it's different. The Internet has truly made a difference, whether you are buying or selling. As a seller, online you now have access to almost the entire global population, and even though that's an exciting prospect for an entrepreneur, the most exciting prospect, as far as I'm concerned as an entrepreneur, concerns resources, even staff. Only last night over dinner, by sharing what I know about employing "virtual staff" based somewhere like the Philippines, I was able to offer some easily implementable advice to a good friend and fellow entrepreneur who owns a group of estate agents. If he acts on my advice it will allow him to reduce the costs in one part of his business by at least 70% and remove about 20% of his overall operating costs, with very little effort and with only small administration changes, within around four weeks. This highlights how valuable ideas from this chapter could be to you, they could be even more valuable.

Right now you could make the decision to shift from being, as they say here in the UK about solo entrepreneurs, a "one man band", to having a team of literally a thousand people there to help you collect and manage data, create content, undertake research, come up with potential solutions to problems, undertake administration, answer phones and just about every other aspect you might need in your quest to transform your idea into a successful and executable business model. In fact the crowd can even run it for you when you correctly structure things to make it a business.

There are many ways to buy human resources on an ad-hoc basis. You could use a site like CrowdFlower.com who, for a fee, will find the right person or people to deliver exactly what you need, even if that's 20,000+ work hours by specialist people in the next 30 days. Yes, that's right – you can go from zero staff and overheads, to having a specialist and very capable workforce that can turn around years' worth of work in days, and, best of all, when you have done what you need to do, you can go back to not having any staff, all without the traditional infrastructure costs, personnel problems and time delays.

The other way to look at the Internet, when it comes to human resources, is to find people in other parts of the world who are very skilled and can work for you, even full-time if you want, but because of their culture and the relative cost of living, their salary may be less than half what it would be in your own country. I have found, for example, a Philippines a good place to find skilled and very conscientious people who will work for me. If that's something you are interested in doing, then I highly recommend that you buy the book Virtual Freedom by Chris Ducker, who is the expert on the subject and a really nice guy too.

With other business interests, I have had offices in India for programming and catalogue production, and with my family's business interests we have an office and team of people in Guangzhou China that look after many products we design and sell here in the UK but have manufactured all across China because of the cost advantage it gives us in our marketplace. Knowing how to work globally is an exceptionally effective way to maximise your profits; in fact it's such an important part of our family's business that we have somebody from the China office now based in our UK head office, whose role is to manage the communication with the China office and the factories there because it's a full-time job, and it's best to have an experienced person with the first-hand knowledge of what we need, and also how the Chinese factories and systems work. Again, I could write a book or two just about my experiences, good and bad, when it comes to working globally and profiting from this opportunity, but in the short space I have here, all I can say is that if it's an option for you, you must investigate and learn about this fantastic opportunity, because it's something that will just get more and more relevant for all entrepreneurs, wherever you are in the world and however large or small your ideas and businesses are.

Talking more about the Internet and the opportunities it presents, you can use more specific crowd sourcing sites like 99 Designs for graphic design work, Freelancer for programming, writing, creative projects, even things like media buying, lead generation and engineering projects. If you want to find specific people for specific tasks, then just look for what you need in Google and you are sure to find it being provided by the "crowd"; and if you can't find what you needed, then you may have stumbled upon a great idea.

But technology and in particular the Internet, as well as providing opportunities, has also provided threats because barriers to entry into markets are lower than ever before, which potentially increases the competition level, again another reason you never want to compete purely on the basis of price.

There are studies that show that technology of all types, not just online, grows and provides opportunities at an exponential level. Computers, robotics and all sorts of other pieces of technology get better, faster and cheaper, year on year, and you have to keep an eye on this because it could be either good or bad for your business and entrepreneurial ideas. But focusing on the positives for the time being, rather than the threats, you will recall

I mentioned exponential improvement. Let me just put some scale to this because, whether it's personal improvement, technological improvement, or even sales and marketing improvement, I think you will find this very powerful and more than a big enough reason to try and achieve, as I suggested earlier in the book, daily improvements of just 1%.

If you think of improvement as a series of steps, just to make it easier to visualise, if you take 30 individual steps towards your goal, you have moved 30 places closer, and that's a positive result, but when you harness the exponential power of things like technology, and take 30 exponential steps, then you don't move 30 places, you move over one billion places – yes, one billion! The thing is, because of what other people are doing, you don't need to invent and develop those exponential steps, you just have to find them, because others with far more resources are providing them for you and you can use your entrepreneurial capabilities to make use of them as and when you want to or need to. The perfect example using other exponential ideas and technological developments is 3D printing, which is set to revolutionise so many things in the next 10 years. I expect 3D printing and variations of it to impact medical science, manufacturing and retail; just imagine what happens when you can download from the Internet a design or program and print what you need to repair or replace items, even complex ones. As you can imagine, things will change, and it's how you identify potential changes and opportunities that will ultimately allow you to flourish as an entrepreneur, and why being a big or even an established business is little or no advantage in the world we now live in.

Things will change faster than ever, and will continue to change at this sort of exponential rate. Just think about simple niche areas like photography – the old-fashioned camera and film is history, as are some of the major companies which once dominated that market, all because of digital photography. And now the digital camera faces challenges, as photographs are taken, edited and shared using your smartphone, and I expect things to continue to change for that market and associated service providers too.

Talking of digital photography, this is a subject very close to my heart because it's something my family were instrumental in helping to develop and commercialise more than 20 years ago. Because of our need to take over 200 photographs a day in our in-house photography studios, we were one of only two organisations that initially worked with hardware and software manufacturers to make it work as a concept, and while people in the photographic industry said it would never work, and the quality would never be good enough, and also because the initial costs were very high, it was a challenge, but it was right for us to move the game on and ultimately we proved to be correct, while in the process reducing our costs by many thousands of pounds a day, which both saved our clients money and increased our productivity and profitability. Digital photography simultaneously helped us win new customers.

Now nobody would dream of not using digital photography, yet 20-odd years ago, we had to work through the technical issues and challenges as well as the marketplace scepticism. History proves we were right, and maybe this is why I am now so passionate about the role technical opportunities play in the life and success of an entrepreneur. By the way, we still have that very first digital camera as a reminder of the past, but the camera out photography studios use now is very, very different, costs a fraction of the amount it used to yet is even better quality – it's a perfect example of what I'm sharing in this chapter.

On the flip side of this exponential opportunity, it's important to understand that people don't change – they still buy benefits, based on emotion more often than on logic and features. What has changed, though, is the speed at which opinions and ideas change, and this is why learning from others and using the right tools, for example social media, crowd funding and crowd sourcing sites, has become so important.

When you are planning, designing, manufacturing, marketing, selling, delivering and supporting the needs of your customer, you always need to be thinking about how best to do this; I recommend you think about using tools such as video, graphics, audio, text and even presentations in the right way to be highly effective and cost effective too. You can even combine two completely different ideas and see vastly improved results – one example and way of doing this is called gamification, where you add a competitive or fun element to something that is not normally seen as fun, when you want people to do something or take action. Gamification has been used as a technique to conduct medical research, find solutions to industrial problems, make people fitter and more healthy, and even to improve our environment, so don't be afraid to think laterally about your ideas, and link what you know from one area or industry with another to see if it can deliver the results you want.

As you can see, by setting aside time to learn, take in and even try new things in your marketplace and in other areas too, you will be able to appreciate and refine potential benefits and opportunities from the vast amount of content there now is on every single subject, and again you can use your skill of failing and failing fast to help here.

I hope you can see how each section of this book is now starting to converge in a way that will make you a more effective entrepreneur. As a summary of this chapter, make sure you are aware of how new technology, new online opportunities and also the global market for people and production can be harnessed, yet also potentially threatening your ideas. This way you are being proactive and using your skill as an entrepreneur who moves the game on, moving ahead of the competition, making money and also growing your results, maybe even growing them exponentially, rather than step-by-step.

The new economy in which we all live, work and sell has a new framework for success, and entrepreneurs are the best-placed people to take advantage of this and profit, as employees and business-owners find it harder and less profitable as time passes. No matter how big your ideas are, or how previously you felt that your goals were out of reach, because the rules of the game have changed, you have the chance to set out new rules and create new or updated games in line with your aspirations.

CHAPTER 9
COMMUNICATING WITH YOUR AUDIENCE

I initially thought the title of this chapter should have been "Marketing to your audience", but when I thought about things, I realised more and more that communicating was a far better word to use. In this chapter I will be explaining the right ways to build a relationship with your prospects, and how to build as efficient a system for generating profitable sales as I can in a single chapter. My challenge however, is to make it as easy for you as I can to learn from my experience in marketing, which as I have said, spans over 20 years of work in traditional and digital media channels, and for all sorts of types of people and companies. At the same time I don't want you to feel overwhelmed, because in reality you will see just how simple, logical and systematic great communication can be. I am also going to help you with more than just sales and marketing, so…

Let me just start with the fact that "audience" is not just another word for prospective customers, even though this is how almost all people see it. Your audience does include prospects, but it also includes people who are not prospects – it includes suppliers, competitors, members of staff, in fact anybody who comes into contact with you and your business. As an entrepreneur, I want to help you apply some psychology to the communication of your ideas and as such do things far more tactically than a design, marketing, advertising or PR agency may suggest, because that's what works best.

Let me just start with a definition of marketing, because that will really help you see what marketing is and what it isn't. The definition I will use is one by Strategic Coach founder, Dan Sullivan:

"Marketing is any activity that gets people intellectually engaged in a future result that's good for them and getting them to emotionally commit to take action to achieve that result."

I also want to say at this point that I don't segment marketing, advertising, PR, or any other promotional activity for that matter, into separate categories; to me, they all come under the umbrella term marketing, and I definitely don't segment traditional and digital forms of marketing. We all have to think and work cross-media because that's the way the world works now, and it will save you a great deal of time, money and effort to think this way.

The other recommendation I want to make at the outset is that you work hard to make sure your communication is effective and well thought out, not just prior to a sale, but at the point of and after the sales process too. This is something I see people and companies fail to do all the time.

My personal experience in every market in which I have ever worked on how good communication affects a business has made several things extremely clear. When I share these with you, as an entrepreneur, I'm sure you will be keen to apply what you learn in this chapter to what you do. The right communication means that:

- You can charge more money.

- You will promote and sell on things other than price.

- Your suppliers and team members will be important assets to you.

- You will influence, maybe even control a market.

- You will have more loyal customers.

- You will have better insight and feedback from the marketplace.

- You will benefit from free publicity and promotion.

- It will be easier to generate repeat custom and referrals.

- You will attract new customers more easily and at a lower cost.

The main goal with all your communication is to build your brand. I don't mean brand in a design and logo sense; to me, as an entrepreneur, marketing and branding is all about attracting the right people to what you do, and repelling the wrong type of people. At the same time, branding gives you the opportunity to develop a strong, positive association with your target audience or market because this creates a situation where you have some standing and are seen as a trusted advisor or supplier for any and all types of product or service you wish to offer; there isn't a scenario I have ever come across where the right marketing and branding doesn't add massive value to a situation, and this in turn gives you the opportunity to build a sustainable and long-term position within your chosen market and to profit from it because you continually move the game on.

There are two factors that will determine if you can be successful. The first is your communication and the second is your ability to deliver on your promises. One without the other will lead to failure; it also highlights your need to get your communication and marketing right.

People have passion – that's what you need to tap into with your communications, but you can't afford to have passion for anything other than adding value to your chosen market. You shouldn't use your passion on a product or service – perhaps this initially sounds wrong, but if you do that then you risk being constrained by the product or service. It's why I said earlier that turning a hobby or passion into a business may not be the best idea.

People buy because of emotions and the benefits you demonstrate to them, rather than features. This is a mistake many people make, and I highly recommend that you only spend your time, money and effort on tangible, emotional benefits. For example, don't sell an exercise bike, or worse still, features on an exercise bike: sell getting fit and healthy and what this will mean to the customer. Such a benefit is less price-sensitive, too.

Another key aspect to your communication is that if you have no passion and energy, this will come across in what you do, so don't be afraid to stop, take a minute to refocus or even stop what you are doing altogether. That way you minimise risk and maximise the chances of success. I also want to mention that you may have others working with you in order to head towards your goals, but as an entrepreneur you have to be the momentum behind the campaign. This is necessary to ensure that you have the ability to direct others involved in all your communication and get the most out of all the time, money and effort you invest, as well as making sure you present a consistent message to the market, which is key for every entrepreneur.

When it comes to any sort of communication, obviously your end goal is a sale, but there are many things you can do to, as I say, "stack the deck in your favour". Let me share some of these with you.

There are four rules of any marketing or communication, if it is to work.

First, the communication must be directed to a person, not a company, who has the potential to buy what you are offering, who can afford to buy or can authorise the purchase of what you are offering, and who would be interested in what you are offering too.

I estimate that over 90% of business communications fail on this one point alone. Just think about direct mail you get that is of no interest to you, the emails and spam that arrive every single day that are just an inconvenience, online adverts that you see on websites you visit that are totally irrelevant, adverts and pieces of PR in newspapers and magazines that are just not applicable, and even TV and radio commercials that are just not for you, for any number of reasons – and that's just the communication you noticed, what about all the things you didn't notice? The people doing this are spending money, even though they have no chance of selling to you – what a waste.

Now I'm not going to suggest that you can have a 100% perfect communication strategy, but the right mailing list, good media buying, effective online marketing and other things will generate far more results and a better return on investment for you and that's why I want you to be able to measure the results of your communication, by using the techniques that are integrated into direct response marketing; more on that later.

Next, the communication must be noticed. You can do this in various ways; some people call this a "pattern interrupt", but simply put, it's all about getting people to stop what they are doing to give you literally a second or two of their time. That way you can pitch your idea to them, and that is why your headline and first impression is so important, whether in print or on digital media platforms.

Third is the fact that, to help your prospect (and that's a key point – to help, not sell to the prospect), the piece of communication must be "consumed". Again, your message quality and effectiveness are the most important factors here.

And finally, the prospect must respond to your call to action, which may or may not be making a sale, but so long as they are moving closer to the point of sale, that's OK.

Let me quickly share with you some of the main principles behind direct response marketing. The priority of importance in what and how you communicate is as follows.

First and most important is the quality of your list or audience. There is no point promoting a product for men to women, or a new Rolls-Royce to people with no money. Simply put, that would be stupid and a waste of your time, money and effort, but I see this sort of mistake happen all the time. Don't take a media owner or media buyer's sales pitch or advice as factually correct; make sure you can assess it yourself.

Next is the effectiveness and quality of your offer. If you have targeted the right people, and what you are offering is compelling, they will take action. If it's only an interesting offer, or you need to try and convince them of what you have, then you will see significantly fewer results from the same expenditure. I regularly see an increase of seven to ten times in results when I get involved with a client's marketing to start with, when they follow these rules.

Third, and least important, is the quality of the creative component of your communication. (I understand that this will upset designers, photographers and people who try and sell creative services, but this is the reality, based on factual results, not theory.) Just because it's third on the list, however, doesn't mean it's not relevant: you just need to invest in it correctly, based on your market's needs and expectations.

When you are about to start planning any form of communication to anybody, you have to start with the following three elements in mind, and they are all from your ideal customer's perspective, not yours:

Where am I now? (Remember, that's from the customer's perspective.)

Where do I want to get to?

What am I prepared to give up to get there? This could be time, money or something else, but it's important to know this.

Based on these three things, here is a simple checklist that a direct response marketing piece of communication must satisfy:

Your offer is specific and unique.

Your offer is easy to understand and buy.

The offer has value to the audience; it's not just useful, so you know they will want it. As I explain to people I work with, the content of your communication has potential, but it's the context of it that gets results for you.

The "promises" you make are plausible. This is really key, because if your prospects cannot see themselves reaching their goals with what you are offering, they will not buy.

There is a level of urgency in the offer.

The offer is guaranteed.

Remember, the great thing about this form of marketing and communication is that whenever you are doing something and spending money, you are able to monitor the results. After your initial low-cost testing, because traffic and prospects are a result of your marketing, the return on the investment is always positive: you never have to spend £1 and not get more than £1 back as a result.

You'll recall that earlier in the book we talked about the integrated product and service suite, so make sure you know how a happy customer will move through your different product and service sales, and the value of a customer too; this is sometimes called customer lifetime value, and will determine how much you can afford to spend acquiring customers. In fact in some cases, businesses can afford to lose money at the customer acquisition phase, based on the average lifetime value each customer represents. Retailers call this type of offering a "loss leader".

Because direct response is designed to get an immediate response from your marketing and communications, one that is specific and quantifiable, it's far easier to not just measure your return on investment, it's also far easier to automate a sales and marketing system, with some careful planning and execution. As much as automation is a whole new subject, indeed more than a book in itself, if you want to make money almost on autopilot, then I suggest looking at online software systems like Infusionsoft, which is what I use, AWeber or GetResponse that help you do this for a just few hundred dollars or less a month.

When it comes to communication, another entrepreneurial tip I always give is that, before you get to the design of your product or service, you actually write a sales letter. This should ensure that, as a minimum, you deliver what your customers want and need with a product or service, especially as, if you recall, you want to sell what people want, but give them what they need. In delivering on this, you will "know" or understand the person you are targeting and will only deal with them if what you have is going to deliver what they need, and only if it makes commercial and moral sense for you too. This is why you will be able to give a good and highly promotable guarantee, because you know the market, you know that what you have is great value, and it works. Having a good guarantee is a fantastic sales proposition.

You probably also remember, way back in Chapter 4 of the book I said, "If you are looking for customers then you are doing the wrong thing. You should always be looking to help people move from where they are now to where they want to be – this is what should shape and influence your product or service design and development, as well as all your promotional activity. This will result in better, more profitable and loyal customers." Well here's what I promised to tell you about, and an example too.

First of all, all your communication needs to attract people you want to work with, and repulse those you do not want to work with, because people who are not right for what you do will take up valuable time, money and effort if you let them. Once you have identified people you want to do business with, maybe now or maybe in the future, you need to be as efficient as possible at managing them, and the best way to do this is by always adding value to them whenever they come into contact with you, or as I call this, at every communication touch point, that's basically anywhere they can see you online, in print, even in person. I want to make sure that as an entrepreneur, all of your communication:

is consistent in message and quality;

is helpful, adding value or even training your prospects, getting them results and closer to where they want to get to for free;

makes bold claims, yet honest too. The best way to keep promises is by not promising something you can't deliver; having a bold guarantee shows you have confidence in your product or service;

is respectful of others, their skills, work, effort, time and money.

Also don't be afraid of being wrong and admitting it, for instance when accepting and learning from failures. It's a good thing to do and will win you support and trust from your chosen marketplace.

I realise that this chapter has many aspects, and even now there is so much more I would like to say, but I know that too much information is just as detrimental as too little, and the aim of this book is for you to take action and start your entrepreneurial journey, if you haven't already; if you have, then I want to make sure you can see and take action on your ideas in the most effective way possible. With those things in mind I want to just do one more thing for you in this chapter, and that's to show you a simple but effective marketing funnel:

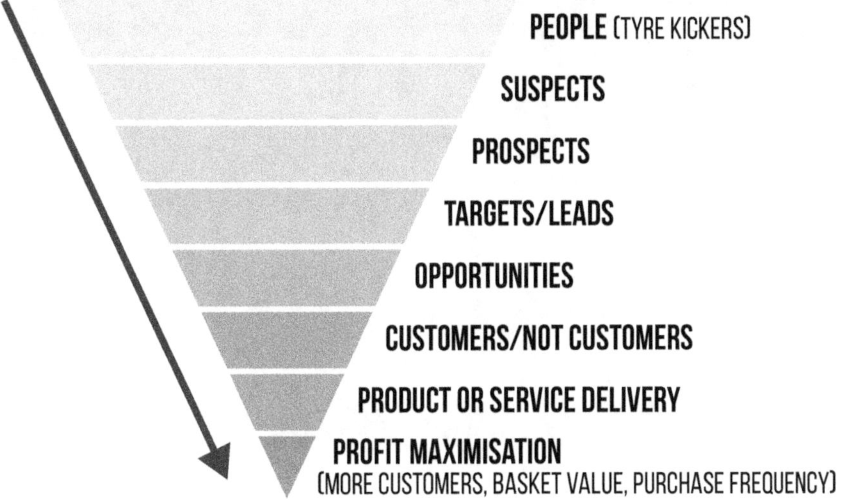

This is how you should plan to move people thorough what you call a marketing funnel. The best thing I can do for you is explain this in a video, so I have created another video for you at **www.theentrepreneursbook.com** which will give you time to think about all the things in this chapter, and also allow you to focus just on this funnel when you watch the video, as it's a very powerful framework that will really allow you to maximise your results and minimise your costs too.

In summary, communication needs to be planned; when done correctly, this is the key to being a successful entrepreneur. Also, when you use direct response marketing principles, you are able to refine what you do so that you are generating the best possible return on investment. This also allows you to focus on what you do best and love the most, which is being an entrepreneur.

CHAPTER 10

DON'T LET OTHERS GET IN YOUR WAY

In all the projects I have ever worked on, the hardest part has always been working with other people. I guess that's because I have a particular set of work ethics, personal ethics, quality standards and, most of all, core values that are my guiding principles, all of which I am proud of and will defend because I believe they are right. But it doesn't mean my guiding principles are the same as other people's and that's just a fact of life and therefore I have to deal with it, just as I do with other things that affect my activities as an entrepreneur. Here lies the issue and challenge, no matter whether people are customers, suppliers, members of my own team, business partners or even friends; what I can say though is that my family share my values and are incredibly supportive, and a great asset to me, but I know of situations other people face where this is not the case, so you may find that family members may also, as I say, get in your way.

In this chapter, I want to share with you not only my tactics for spotting and dealing with people who are not helping, supporting and energising you along your entrepreneurial journey, but also my own experiences, as these can help you and also help you appreciate that even though it sometimes feels lonely being an entrepreneur, in fact you're not alone, and the issues you face have been conquered by others in the past, so don't worry, or worse still, give up on your dreams.

Let me start with a guiding principle that I always work to. It often requires me to take tough decisions and make changes along the way, as you will see later, but if this rule is always applied, in my experience you can't go far wrong, so here it is:

Only work with those you trust and respect.

When working with others, no matter whether they are customers, suppliers or team members, just by tying this rule in to my other defining rule about only doing things I want to do or am paid to do, I've ended up with a pretty compelling and powerful base to operate from as an entrepreneur. It's not just a plan that provides me with the best possible chance of making money, it's also the best strategy if I want to be happy too. Maybe this rule, or a version of it, will work as well for you too?

Let's start by talking about customers; they often seem to think that the phrase "the customer's always right" is actually true. As I'm sure you will agree, they are not always right.

When you are doing your best to add value to customers, to do a great job for them, and a commercially viable job for you too, it's critical that all parties have a mutual respect for each other's skills and expertise and that the trust is there. This makes a potential outcome a win-win scenario. I can't tell you the number of times, in a sales and marketing situation especially, when people will want take as much value from you as they can, in some cases get you to do their job for them too, and not pay you a penny for it. That to me is not a win-win deal, and as such is only going to lead to a strained and less than fruitful relationship. Here's a crazy thing to say, but it's completely true and the main reason I have managed to save at least 12 hours a week of work time and over £2,000 a month in travel costs: I don't go to meetings unless I want to or am paid to; nevertheless, meetings with potential customers have to happen at a certain point in a relationship and when face-to-face dialogue will really move the relationship on, because there is only so much that can be done on the phone, via email or by things like Skype or video conference.

Because the UK is a relatively small place, people here seem to like to have meetings. I also think it's a way for them to exert authority over suppliers and potential suppliers, and if I'm really honest, I think that too many people like meetings because they think it shows that they are doing something, and it makes them feel busy and important, but maybe I'm just being unfair – I'll let you decide. I like to have a pre-defined goal set out to all involved before I attend a meeting – if I want a chat, I can do that with friends. A pre-defined goal is useful if I want or need to explain something to somebody; that way we keep the meeting short, to the point, and with certain expectations on both sides. This often seems counter-intuitive to many people, but I always want to make progress; it's what you and I, as entrepreneurs, thrive on, so that's how I like to manage things. I will admit that I'm not a fan of a full-blown agenda, although sometimes it's necessary for longer meetings with multiple points to cover and progress, but a quick email to all involved is all that it takes, it also ensures that the required people attend the meeting – I can't tell you the number of times I have made the mistake of going to meetings and finding a key person is not present. To me, that is disrespectful of my time and that of others in the meeting.

Obviously I always want to treat people I come into contact with the way I would want to be treated, and as I have said, I also want to enable people to make money and profit too, so let me share with you an example of a situation where a customer completely failed to live up to my expectations – not because the people I worked with were not nice people, but because their values were not the same as mine, and after a single job, I saw the mistakes, the lack of an open an honest relationship and their inability to capitalise on what they could have done, because of their way of working.

As I mentioned earlier in the book, I have some experience in publishing, including my own magazine business interests. I have worked with publishers of newspapers and other magazines, and my goal is always to help them do a better job, to take advantage of opportunities and ultimately make more money (easier said than done in traditional publishing these days). Regarding one particular business opportunity after years of investment, I decided to literally "put my money where my mouth was" for the big newspaper and magazine publishers, because I could see the market opportunity, the fear publishers had, as well as the concerns they had with resources, so I changed our sales and marketing pitch to be something along the lines of this: "We will provide you with the system and the infrastructure to do this for you, we will provide the staff and the technology, and all you need to do is let us help your advertising and sales team make money from the opportunity. In fact we will even have somebody go to sales meetings with your team so that we can speed up the sales process and get your people and your clients up to speed too. We will do most of the work for you, and bearing in mind that what we will be doing for you won digital innovation of the year at the national newspapers awards, it's a proven solution that your advertising clients and readership want, so for no real risk or cost, all we want is for you to give us about 25% of the revenue generated, bearing in mind this is not revenue you get now or could you get either in the next couple of years."

The upshot of the deal was that we started working with one publishing group on a pilot. To say they were in a position to make money was an understatement; in fact as a UK daily national newspaper, we estimated the revenue, once things were organised, which would take less than six weeks, would be in excess of £20,000 a day. So just on one of the newspapers they owned, they could generate an additional £7 million a year, from which they would need to pay us about 25% of that as our fees – not bad for the newspaper, as it was over £5.5 million in what I call "free money", inasmuch as they had to do very little work and invest next to nothing to get it.

Together we created the pilot and actually, if I recall correctly, on day one, generated more than the target £20,000 per day revenue stream; but here comes the issue: I found out that they planned to try and negotiate a seven-figure deal with a sponsor for the service, without getting us involved or paying us part of that fee. They were not transparent or working in the way we had agreed, and as such, the relationship ended because of the lack of trust, so instead of a win-win deal we both lost out, which was a risk I knowingly took, and it was an expensive risk too.

Unfortunately that's not the only time that I have seen customers try to see what they can get away with, and so I always go into situations looking to build trust, first and foremost because when you have that, you can work with each other and build the respect and relationship. On the flip-side of less that perfect business relationships is the fact that I can say, even with companies I no longer work with, some people within those companies I still have a great deal of respect for and will, I hope, work together with again one day, just maybe without the other people who got in the way of the opportunity. What I have realised, and I hope you do too, is that I know the type of people and businesses I want to work with, and those that I don't. I am an entrepreneur and I have set my expectations high, and I work best with entrepreneurial people and companies who will take action and want to move their own game on, so the faster I can identify when a customer or a decision-maker in that organisations is entrepreneurial, the better.

You may have noticed I keep using the word customer, not client, which some of you may find strange. Here's how I define customers and clients. Customers buy something from you. Clients want you to work with them, which there is nothing inherently wrong with, but I don't like having clients, I much prefer to skip this stage and work with partners – these are people you can build a long-term win-win relationship with, sharing the ups and downs. Simply put, by buying this book you became a customer, and I'm not only really pleased you invested in it and thank you for being a customer, but I also would like you to get as much value as possible from it, because that's what I want you to get from your investment of time, money and effort; I don't, however, want you as a client; but just wait a moment as I explain myself.

If you decide you want to work with me more in the future, and I hope you do, I would like it if you became what I term a partner, as then we will be working towards a win-win situation, with trust and respect for each other. I know the distinction between client and partner is perhaps only a matter of semantics, but to me it's really important. I highly recommend that you take time to understand, appreciate and formalise the way you select people to work with in your chosen marketplace. This strategy helps you with your marketing and communication, as you want to be as effective and efficient as you can to attract customers and potential partners, while repelling those you don't want to work with, so that they don't take up your valuable time, money and effort.

Let's move on from customers, and think about people you work with, not just employ; this includes suppliers too. I believe you should find and work with people who share values as close to your own as possible, as it makes for a good working relationship, and this is never more relevant than those you work with day-to-day. There are various ways to see if you will work well with somebody. I'm not going to pretend I am a human resources expert, but something I have found really useful and powerful too, and which is a great way to help build a great team of people to work with, is something called a Kolbe test. I found out about this as a member of Strategic Coach, but if you go to Kolbe.com you will be able to find out more about it. In simple terms, a Kolbe test provides a clear indication of how individuals work and what they are naturally more inclined to do well, so it's ideal for developing and communicating as effectively as possible with a team of people. By the way, my Kolbe score is 4393; when you find out about the test and apply my score to it, you will see why I do what I do, and why I'm an entrepreneur at heart.

I always like to give people the chance to prove themselves. Remember, nobody's perfect either – not even me, as I'm sure others will tell you, because I can be very opinionated and determined sometimes, which is not always what others respond well to. But if you can work with and surround yourself with people who add value, want to make your life easier and who also share your passion, enthusiasm and desire, then you're much more likely to succeed; and if you don't, then expect a harder time than you need to endure.

The best piece of advice I have ever been given on the subject of working with others was from my mother, who always told me: "Do the best job you can to make sure the next person in the process has as easy a job as they possibly can, but don't do their job for them." This is what I try to do, and what I would like those I work with to do too. Just as an example, from earlier this week (and as you will see, it doesn't have to be difficult to do), instead of giving somebody in my office an address for a meeting they were going to, I went to Google maps and printed out the details, as well as the address, showing how they could walk in less than six minutes from the train station they were arriving at to the office they were meeting in. You see, small things to make somebody else's job or life easier can go a long way to building a good working relationship and minimising stress.

Another piece of advice I want to share with you, that I have found really valuable especially with people you work with, is if you are struggling to solve a problem or come up with a plan, using a change of environment or change of activity often helps your mind re-focus and, as a result, come up with potential solutions. This works well not just when you are on your own – doing this with people you work with is an excellent problem-solving strategy. As I work very closely with my father at times, I tend to find that a walk with him and my dog Jimmy on a Sunday allows us to chat in a more relaxed way, and the outcome is that we often have a more productive and fruitful discussion than we ever could in the office. That's also one of the other reasons why I don't believe that being an entrepreneur is a Monday to Friday, 9 to 5 activity. You should take advantage of opportunities whenever they arise, not based on a calendar.

As I have said before, I am fortunate that my friends and family are supportive of my entrepreneurial approach to work. Even on a personal level I am driven and focused on making things work as well as they can – for example with my motor racing, where I always want to apply my constant improvement mentality to what I do. Some people are not as fortunate as me when it comes to supportive friends and family, but all I can say is that friends and family are my priority in life. If that is not so relevant to you, you can help yourself by finding groups of people to work with, socialise with, learn from and even just talk with who understand you. I highly recommend finding mastermind groups or even like-minded people through websites like meetup. com, so there are people who you can bounce ideas off. Other things you will find really helpful are tools like podcasts and audiobooks, even online training courses, so check out iTunes for relevant material and also places like AppSumo.com and Udemy.com for online courses that will help you, not just learn new things, but that also support you as an entrepreneurial person.

Last but not least, I have found it challenging to find business partners to work with, and on more than one occasion I have cut my losses because I did not have the respect and trust in people, and I did not want to be held back by them. The most stressful example of cutting my losses, and the most costly for me too, not just in money but in confidence, was the TV and entertainment project I mentioned back in Chapter 2, that I managed to take from being an idea to the point of obtaining agreed funding to the tune of over $10 million. I will share with you in the next chapter an elevator pitch outline of this project, and another project's elevator pitch too, because I want you to see how ideas, when they are developed correctly, can be "put on ice"; this allows you to make hard decisions for the right reasons, at the right time, without giving up on them. But the very short version of the story was that the whole project was – and still is – a revolutionary idea for the entertainment world. A venture capital fund in Luxembourg agreed and signed a letter of intent to fund it; they even brought in advisors and experts, for whom I still have a great deal of trust and respect, and that would have added massive value to the project. The thing was, though, they were never 100% open with me and my team; they also never acted with the speed they had promised, and the trust was lost. I also was never sure about these people's motives or sources of finance; in fact there were suggestions, which emerged when one of the advisors who they brought to the table, who was very well connected in the country, did some background research, that the money was not from a legitimate source. Needless to say, I do not and never will get involved with people I can't trust, so I cut my substantial losses.

I have also had to make tough decisions regarding other business relationships. Many people say they want to work hard and profit from that hard work, effort and the ideas you work on together, but when it comes to the crunch, saying something and doing something can be very different matters. It takes a certain type of person to live up to their promises and more importantly their ability too. For us all, when we don't see immediate results it's hard, so most people tend to worry, and when they lose the confidence with which they set out on their entrepreneurial journey, they give up. Other times, people "self-sabotage" when they start to see the signs of success, which they automatically fear, so watch out for that with others you may work with. I don't ever want to put you off being an entrepreneur, because I believe it's the best possible way to live your life and take control of your own situation, now and in the future, but the simple fact of the matter, as I have said before, is that it will never be easy.

As an entrepreneur you will have the best of times and worst of times, so you need to be clear in your own mind that those you work with as customers, suppliers, staff or in any other capacity, must never manipulate you to the point where you give up on your dreams. You have to be committed and able to demonstrate to others, maybe even persuade them too, that what you are doing is right, and you will not give up until you reach your goals. Also, don't judge your own situation based on the appearance, as opposed to the reality, of others; think of being an entrepreneur as being like a swan – graceful to the outside world, hectic below the surface. The reality is that every entrepreneur wants to be seen in the best possible light, and appear successful to the outside world; the reality is you also need to accept that being hectic at certain times, in private of course, is also part of the process.

CHAPTER 11

WHAT TO DO NEXT

"If information was all that is needed, everybody would be skinny, rich and happy."

I decided to start and end this chapter with a quote; this first one is from Les Brown, one of the world's leading motivational speakers. This is the final chapter, and I'm incredibly pleased and humbled by the fact that you are still with me, because most people don't follow through. The fact that you are still here shows that you are one of the very small percentage of people who do, and that signifies to me that you can and most likely will be a successful entrepreneur, if that's still your intention; I hope what I have shared with you in this book hasn't put you off, and the advice and personal experiences I have shared serve you well in whatever you decide to do next.

I promised in the last chapter that I would tell you more about the TV and entertainment project. What I have decided to do, just to give you more of an insight to how my entrepreneurial mind works, is create an elevator pitch for a couple of what I consider to be game-changing ideas.

Sometimes other commitments can prevent you from taking entrepreneurial ideas to market, in the short term at least. If you organise and plan things correctly, however, you can actually come back to ideas when it suits you; and in some cases that's a very astute tactic because, as with the first elevator pitch for the TV and entertainment project, the cost of delivering it to market is now only about 10 to 20% of the original cost, because of the technological and social media developments since it was first conceived.

By the way, if either of these ideas are something that you would like to find out about, and maybe even become involved in on a win-win basis, then please feel free to get in touch; I hope you appreciate that, if you are the type of person that I love to work with, then there's no telling what might happen. Each idea is much more developed than the elevator pitch shows; simply put, I never intended to use this book as a way to pitch an idea or to give away ideas that I have, but I do want to help you. Understanding ideas and also having an elevator pitch for all of your ideas is really useful; it may even be the thing to do next, so sharing some of my own I hope helps.

So here goes with the first idea, the TV and entertainment project known internally as "String Media".

Imagine an episode of a show like "24", where you can actually influence what happens, almost in real time. Think about what it would feel like to not just watch a TV show, but all of a sudden appear in it, genuinely blurring the worlds of fictional TV, reality TV and real life.

Think about what happens when a TV show not only fully embraces the second screen experience and social media in a way that allows people to share their opinions and be entertained, but also changes entertainment expectations, as you never deliver a show that is anything other than what an audience wants.

The guiding principle of String Media has always been to provide a compelling, inclusive, cross-media entertainment platform that delivers for the audience and also provides a unique and unrivalled level of insight and commercial value for brands and those that "love data", so in fact traditional TV companies may not be the best people to deliver this to the market, because it's so much more than a TV show.

What was pioneering in 2008 is now much easier, and having worked with and developed technology that radically reduces the cost of delivering such a project across smartphones, tablet devices and social media, the String Media platform today now has a delivery cost of less than 20% of the initial budget. Added to this, the production process is far, far faster, making almost real-time engagement-led entertainment a possibility.

Traditional TV and entertainment is based on what I, and many others, believe is an outdated and broken platform. String Media is what people want – nobody has been able to deliver it to them, but it's just a matter of time before we do.

That's String Media, but let me give you something else, called the Opinion Engine. It's different but also game-changing and something I get really excited about every time I revisit it, so here goes.

We have all used a search engine, but opinions are what matters most, because it's people's opinions that enable us to take information and turn it into something relevant, actionable and valuable.

When people plug in the Opinion Engine to their websites, blogs, social media accounts, surveys, even their offline media content too, it becomes possible to translate structured and unstructured data from any and all sources, all the way from a single Tweet to the results based on behaviour and information gathered from across millions of news and information websites, in a way that makes it easy to access and appreciate, just like a search engine. But the Opinion Engine is equally specific and even more powerful for those that want to learn more on a bespoke topic from an open or closed but potentially significant sized user group.

The Opinion Engine provides you with the genuine feelings and real opinions of people in a way that can never be obtained from surveys or research, and at a scale and speed that will revolutionise everything from politics to what you wear for a night out, from investment in new business ideas to the needs of those in need. It's free to get those opinions too, just as it is when you use a search engine.

The Opinion Engine can do for decision-making what Google and others have done for providing access to information, and as such it's a compelling and powerful tool that will be a catalyst for exponential growth of people and businesses almost immediately when launched.

So there you have a couple of my big ideas. As I mentioned before sharing these ideas, I want you to think about how to put your ideas into an elevator pitch, because it's a great thing to do, and inspirational, too. It also means you can explain your idea to anybody, no matter who they are or what they do, in a very short space of time, which is a valuable skill for you to master.

Before I finish, I want to try and summarise over 34,000 words in just a few lines for you. Here goes.

As an entrepreneur, when you are about to start or even if you are already doing something, ask yourself:

- Where am I now in relation to my goals?

- Where do I want to get to?

- What's the purpose of this?

- Does it move the game on?

- Why should I do it?

- What's the ideal outcome?

- What am I prepared to give up to get to where I want to be?

When you are looking to move your idea from being just that in to being a business, make sure that you:

- think about the value of your product or service to the target market;

- undertake due diligence and research to minimise risk;

- think about the price and make sure it's profitable;

- produce pre-production samples or test out your service, but keep costs under control;

- design marketing and communication that is clear, concise and effective by using direct response principles;

- create your actual product or commercialise your service and make sure it works as a business so you are not key to it operating, so that you can remain an entrepreneur, not just become a business-owner;

- continue to improve your product or service as often as you can to stay ahead of the market.

And remember, to create a successful company you must operate in a profitable niche and have a consistent and predictable flow of new customers. Remember also that once people are customers, you can and should sell them more than one thing, through a pre-defined integrated product or service suite.

There are just three more things to say before I get to the quote which I shall use to end this book. The first is, please let me know how you get on, your successes and challenges, and also what you thought of the book. That is really important to me, because my goal is to add as much value as I can to people who share my passion for being an entrepreneur. You can do this via the contact area at the theentrepreneursbook.com members' area.

Second, make sure you have gone to theentrepreneursbook.com and registered for the video training, because not only will you get that, I will also make sure I keep you updated with new ideas, tactics and frameworks that will be easy to learn and apply in whatever you decide to do with your entrepreneurial talents. I know, based on your being at this point of the book, that I can help and support you as you become a very successful entrepreneur. Also, from time to time, especially here in the UK, as I feel there is a lack of support for people like you and I here, I'll be arranging mastermind sessions and events that I would love you to join. I also create training programmes for entrepreneurs and occasionally speak in the UK and overseas at large events and for private groups on the subjects of marketing and entrepreneurship, so I want to give you access to these too when I can, because I know they will help if you are looking to accelerate your results. You can also find me on Twitter, my username, not surprisingly, is @AdrianFleming.

And one last thing before the quote: if you feel you would like to work with me on a one-to-one basis, or in a small group situation, as these are the best ways for me to really help you, where I do my best work and also provide as much value as I can, I'd love to hear from you. However I have to let you know, I don't work with everybody – I can't from a time point of view, but more importantly, I focus on only working with those people I can add the most value to in the shortest possible time; however, as somebody who's at this point in the book, you seem like that type of person, so feel free to make contact via my website AdrianFleming.com.

Now we are at the end, and the reason for ending on a quote (in fact it's more of an urban legend than a 100% accurate and attributable quote) is this: if you only take one message from this book, then it should be this and I hope a little bit of humour will help you remember it too – if you follow the information in this book I am confident that you will make your life as an entrepreneur, as easy and rewarding as it can be. Reading the book and doing your best is no guarantee of success, but this quote, from a chap called Willie Sutton, who died back I 1980s, even though his choice of profession is not in line with my values, shows there was logic and reasoning behind what he did. It makes a great deal of sense, it also reminds me, and I hope you too, that by doing certain things, you can stack the odds in your favour. Knowing your goals and having a plan is key and, just as Willie found out on many occasions, even though you will not always get the result you want every time, and will experience setbacks, that's part of being an entrepreneur too. It's how you rebound from a setback that defines you as a person and as an entrepreneur.

Thank you again and I hope to hear about your own journey as an entrepreneur, and meet you in person one day.

Here's Willie's quote…

"The reason I rob banks is because that's where the money is."

www.ingramcontent.com/pod-product-compliance
Lightning Source LLC
Chambersburg PA
CBHW061005050726
47592CB00003B/1353